# BUSINESS INTUITION

UPLEVEL YOUR INTUITION, TAP INTO
YOUR INNER WISDOM, AND BECOME THE
ENTREPRENEUR YOU WERE MEANT TO BE

HOLLY E. WORTON

# CONTENTS

*Business Intuition: Tools to Help You Trust Your Own Instincts, Connect with Your Inner Compass, and Easily Make the Right Decisions*

**by Holly E Worton**

A CIP catalogue record for this book is available from the British Library

ISBN 978-1-911161-66-0 Kindle
ISBN 978-1-911161-67-7 EPUB
ISBN 978-1-911161-68-4 Paperback

First edition: 2016
Second edition: 2020

Published by Tribal Publishing Ltd

Please direct permissions requests to:
permissions@tribal-publishing.com

# INTRODUCTION TO THE FIRST EDITION

*"Faith is taking the first step even when you don't see the whole staircase."*

— MARTIN LUTHER KING, JR.

Earlier this year, I mapped out all the books I wanted to write and publish this year. I have a notebook with a list of book titles that I'm constantly adding to whenever a new book idea pops into my mind. I keep a list on one page, and then I write each book title onto a Post-It, which I paste onto the facing page. This makes it easy for me to move around each book and adjust its estimated release date.

I like to keep things flexible, which is a good thing. *Business Intuition* was much farther down on my list of books to release. It was actually an add-on, by which I mean that it wasn't in the initial list of books I planned to publish in 2016. But there was a point where I got the gut feeling that I needed to write and release this book before my bigger *Business Mindset* book, and so I shifted things around so I could release this book in September.

But then I got a second gut feeling about my *Downs Link* walking book that was originally supposed to be released in August, and I swapped the release dates for that book and this one. My intuition told me that writing this book was much more urgent than releasing either the *Downs Link* book or the *Business Mindset* one. And so I trusted it, even though my head wasn't sure exactly what was going on.

I also got a second gut feeling about my *Downs Link* walking book: I had originally walked the trail from north to south, and suspected that the walk might be even better if done from south to north. My intuition whispered to me, "Why don't you walk it one more time, from south to north, before you finish the book?" I realized that would make for a much more interesting and useful book, and I quickly scheduled it into my calendar.

This book is a bit different from my previous three business books: *Business Visibility: How to Transform Your Business Mindset & Increase Your Visibility*, *Business Beliefs: 600+ Beliefs That Make Up a Successful Business Mindset*, and *Business Blocks: How to Identify and Release Your Blocks to Create a Successful Business Mindset*. Those titles focused on how to create a mindset full of business beliefs which serve you and help you to build your business, while at the same time identifying and releasing the mindset blocks that might stop you from achieving your business goals. The first three books are complementary to this one, and are not a prerequisite to understanding the concepts included in this book. You can read the books in any order you like.

This particular book looks at a completely different aspect of business mindset: intuition. Though to be honest, I'm not even sure if intuition can be considered an aspect of mindset, or whether it's an entirely separate thing. Mindset is more about attitudes and beliefs. But to me, intuition plays a massive part in how I build and run my business, and I'm very excited to be writing this book.

As you can see from my story above, I chose this as the topic for my next book because my "gut" told me to do so. They say that you teach what you most need to learn, and it's been a very long process for me to reconnect with my inner wisdom and listen to my intuition. It was silent for so many years, and I felt so out of touch with myself.

But now I've managed to tap into my intuition and reap the benefits of its wisdom, and I'm very excited to share with you how you can learn to do this, too. I didn't have a system or a method when I started to focus on my intuition, and I think that's what made it such a long, difficult process.

Intuition is like a flashlight that shows us the next step or steps on our path toward our business goals. It gives us the confidence to take the next step and start walking down the path, even when we can't see the entire journey from here to our goals. When I don't follow my intuition, I feel like I'm fumbling around in the dark. When I do follow it, I'm confident in the actions that I take.

I've written these mindset books to help you get clarity on the specific things that are holding you back from growing your business. If you're not paying attention to your intuition, that can make building your business so much harder. In this book, I'll share with you some tips that I've learned along the way, in the hopes that they will help you to reconnect with your inner wisdom more quickly and easily than I did. Because I'm all about making things as easy as possible.

# INTRODUCTION TO THE SECOND EDITION

There is a voice that doesn't use words. Listen.

— RUMI

This is the fourth and final book in my Business Mindset series. In 2020, I set out to update all four books, which were originally only available as ebooks. Now, they're available as ebooks, paperbacks, audiobooks, and workbooks. I know that different people have different preferences, and I'm pleased to make the books easier for everyone to read.

I received great feedback over the years about all four books, but I always had it in mind to update them—and not just to publish the books in new formats. Since 2016 when I released my first books, I've become a better writer. I've also worked with more clients and I have more experience with business mindset. My intuition is stronger than ever, and it continues to be an important part of my life—and business.

Intuition is an important part of my business. I often say that my gut is smarter than my head. I find that when I make gut-based decisions, things work out well and I get great results. But when I let my head get in the way, it doesn't always work out the way I want it to. That's why I believe that intuition is an important part of business—and life.

Let's get started!

## 1

# PURPOSE OF THIS BOOK

*"Never apologize for trusting your intuition -- your brain can play tricks, your heart can blind, but your gut is always right."*

— RACHEL WOLCHIN

### What I want

I have a couple of intentions for this book. First, that it will help you understand what it means to fully trust your intuition and how you can harness the power of your inner wisdom in your business so you can create major shifts in how you operate as an entrepreneur. Second, that it will encourage you to exercise your intuition muscle by paying attention to it and taking action on the messages that it gives you.

Why? Because, as the quote above explains, your intuition will never lead you down the wrong path. It's the finest business mentor you'll ever have, because it knows best. You've always got it with you, and it's free! We all come with intuition pre-loaded onto the hard drives of our minds.

Learning to listen to my intuition and then take action on its advice has been life- and business-changing for me, and it's helped me to make decisions to do things that my head would never have encouraged. It's such a powerful tool, and I want you to have easy access to your intuition, too. I firmly believe that if all entrepreneurs listened to and took action on the things that their intuition told them to do, they'd be able to run their businesses more easily and effortlessly.

I believe that building a successful business requires a lot of work, but I'm not a fan of *hard* work. Instead, I believe that growing a business can involve an effortless feeling of flow rather than the stressful feeling that we can get from hustling all the time. And with this book, I hope to show you that this is possible.

Before I go on, I feel the need to really make it clear that business *does* involve work. I'm not implying that all you have to do is to sit back, relax, and listen to your intuition and your business will magically build itself with a little bit of fairy dust. What I mean is that it can be *easier* once you get on board with what your intuition has to say.

As I mentioned earlier, it took me many years to be able to go inward and listen to my gut feeling when it spoke to me. I hope that this book will make the process easier for you. I'm all about doing things the easy way, while taking steady inspired action toward my goals. My first company was super stressful, and I've vowed never to run another business like that again.

You may be wondering, what's inspired action? It's those tasks and action steps that feel totally aligned and right for us. Often, the inspiration for these actions comes from our gut feeling, or intuition, which is why they feel so aligned.

## What do you want?

But let's focus on *you* for a minute. And let's start with the end in mind. What exactly do *you* want to get out of reading this book? What are *you* hoping to achieve? Why do you want to improve your business intuition? What do you hope it will bring to your life?

Stop reading for a minute, think about this, and then write down your answer somewhere. It's important to know what you want to get out of this book, because it means you'll be more likely to achieve it. It's also important to write it down, for three reasons: it helps you to clarify your intentions, it helps you to commit to these intentions, and it helps you to see whether you have achieved these goals once you've finished reading this book.

I often encourage people to start a journal or notebook, or record their thoughts in a file on their computer. This helps you to make note of all the discoveries that you have as you're reading. This book is meant not meant as entertainment: I'm hoping that it will help you make a major shift in your life by encouraging you to listen to the messages your intuition gives you and take action on them, and in order for this to happen, you're going to need to do some work. It doesn't just happen magically; not for me nor for anyone I've ever spoken with on this topic.

Are you ready to delve deeper into the world of business intuition? I hope so. How exciting! I'm seriously excited to take you on this journey. I never considered myself to be an intuitive person before, but now I do. And you can be, too! Ready to get started?

**You're in the right place if:**

- You've ever made a bad business investment, whether it was an expensive business coach/mentor, an online program, or something else. You regret that decision, and you wonder how you could have thought that was the right thing for you at that time.
- You've ever had a bad feeling about a new project that your business mentor encouraged you to take on, but went through with it anyway because you believed she knew best, only to have it flop in the end. Afterwards, you were left kicking yourself and wondering what went wrong.
- You've ever listened to a business buddy's advice about what you needed to do to grow your business more quickly, even though it didn't seem right, and later regretted your decision. And then you wondered, if it worked for her, why didn't it work for you?
- You've ever felt stuck and frustrated because you had absolutely no idea what to do in a particular situation, and then ended up making the wrong decision. It made you feel even more frustrated, because you spent time carefully considering the pros and cons of each option, and even then it didn't work out in your favor.
- You've ever had a great idea for something, but then your head got in the way, and you now regret never taking action on it.

As with my previous three business mindset books, I've

intentionally kept this book short so you can use it as a quick, practical reference to transform your business intuition, and not get caught up in lots of theory. This book is all about getting clarity fast, and then taking action on what you've learned. I'm a big believer that *you* know what's best for you, so I encourage you to use this book in whatever way you find most useful. If you have any questions, please get in touch via my website: www.hollyworton.com.

If you have any questions, please get in touch via my website: www.hollyworton.com.

## 2

# MY JOURNEY TO INTUITION

*"Your intuition knows what to do. The trick is getting your head to shut up so you can hear."*

— LOUISE SMITH

For many years, I was a business mindset coach for women entrepreneurs. I worked with women who were feeling stuck and frustrated because they felt like they were hitting a plateau in their business. Maybe they were struggling to get a steady stream of clients, or maybe they wanted to grow their business to a new level. My work was to help them release their fear of visibility, set aligned prices for their products and services, and take inspired action to grow their business.

Today, I've taken a step back from one-to-one sessions so I can focus on my writing. I've learned a lot from years of coaching and mindset work with clients that I want to share in a bigger way through my books.

Intuition is a very important part of my business and life. It helps me to instinctively know which decisions to make in my business, and which actions to take. It helps me to trust myself and to not waste time evaluating the pros and cons of different situations. It helps me to understand when I need to say no to certain things, so I can have the time and energy to take on projects that are an easy yes.

But it wasn't always this way. In fact, I've only started paying attention to my intuition in the past few years. Before that, I felt horribly lost and confused, unable to know what was best for me. I felt terribly out of touch with myself and disconnected from myself. It was like I was a stranger in my own mind.

It's important for me to tell you a little bit more about my story so you can understand one very important concept: intuition is like a muscle. The more you use it, the stronger it gets. If you currently feel out of touch with yourself, like your intuition doesn't even exist, that's fine. There is hope for you! Hearing the messages from your intuition is a skill you can learn, not something that you're either born with or you aren't. We've all got our own sense of intuition; whether it's strong or weak depends on how much we pay attention to it or how much we ignore it.

### My first business

I started my first company in 1999, with a business partner. We were very different people and had very different skill sets and levels of entrepreneurial experience: for me, it was my first business, and for him, it was just one in a string of businesses he had owned and operated. I was thrown into the operation of the business from the start, and I felt very much out of place and over my head with what I was doing. I felt very, very unqualified to be a business owner.

I was learning new things on a daily basis, and was implementing what I learned shortly after. Some aspects of the business I learned as a result of doing things the wrong way, learning from my mistakes. Remember, this was in the early days of the internet, so there wasn't as much information available as there is now. It was a massive growth period for me, one that went on for the ten and a half years I ran the business with my partner.

Because the business was in a constant state of growth and expansion, that meant the same for me. It was hugely transformative on a personal and professional level, but also extremely frustrating and exhausting. I'm very grateful for the experience because I learned so much about business and marketing, but it was truly a trial by fire.

In addition, my business partner and I had very different values, and decisions made based on his values regularly conflicted with my own sense of integrity. I found myself in a position where I allowed decisions to be made that felt completely out of alignment for me.

## The disconnect began

Eventually, after some time of this, I felt so disconnected from myself that I had no idea which way was up, in terms of my own internal compass. So many things felt wrong, and as a coping mechanism I attempted to focus solely on my own area of the business—marketing and advertising—while avoiding the other areas of the company that didn't feel right. It made me feel like I had some level of control.

Still, the company was much bigger than my little area, and it was impossible to ignore the things that didn't feel right. I expanded my coping mechanism to include numbness, to avoid feeling the ickiness of the situation I was in. This made it easier to get through the day to day operation of the business, but it also served to distance me even more from my intuition.

Ten and a half years later, when I quit running the company and left it to my business partner, I was so lost and out of touch with myself that I didn't know what I wanted. All I knew was that I no longer wanted to be running a business with my partner, even though I dearly loved the people who worked for us and I felt terrible about abandoning them. I was very clear on what I *didn't* want—which was one more month in my company—but I had no idea what I *did* want.

## A new beginning

I ended up taking a sabbatical from business, which turned into a year and a half break. During that time, I worked on my personal blog, writing about my cooking and knitting adventures, and I spent a lot of time recovering from the stress and burnout of my first company. It was a time of letting go of the past and making space for something new, even if I had no idea what that new thing was.

During my sabbatical, I played around with different projects and thought about ideas for a new business. Nothing seemed quite right. I still had that sense of what I *didn't* want, but I still hadn't developed an idea of what I *did* want. Cultivating my intuition was a long process for me, mainly because I had become so disconnected from it for so many years.

Eventually, I moved from Argentina to England, and I still felt lost. I knew I wanted to start another company, but I still didn't know what, so I began applying for jobs in the meantime. But because I had been self employed for over ten years, it was incredibly difficult to find a job.

On one hand, I had so many skills and so much experience, but on the other hand, those skills and experience didn't really translate into a coherent job description. I applied for jobs ranging from online marketing manager to hotel manager to spa director, because I had experience in all of those areas. I had a number of different CVs set up, one for each type of job I was applying for, because if I had written one that fully expressed all of my skills, it would have looked ridiculous to any hiring manager.

I knew that I would be able to do a great job at any of the positions I applied for, but I also knew that I wasn't really excited about any of them. I had interviewed hundreds of people over the course of ten and a half years at my own company, so I knew what to do when I was on the other side of the interview. On the surface level, I interviewed well, but deep down my heart wasn't really in it.

Now, years later, I am so deeply grateful that I didn't get any of those jobs. Yes, I would have performed well. But they would have been soul-sucking and I probably would have spiraled down into a pit of depression.

## Rekindling the connection

Eventually, I discovered coaching. In 2011, I trained as a coach and as an NLP practitioner, and started to build a new company while still applying for jobs at the same time. I knew it would take time to build my new business from scratch, and I needed to have some kind of income in the meantime.

The more coaching training I did, the more I reconnected with myself. In 2013, I trained in a technique called PSYCH-K®, which helps you to reprogram your beliefs at the subconscious level, allowing you to release fears, blocks, and limiting beliefs and reinforce positive, enhancing beliefs. This allowed me to declutter a lot of things that no longer served me and it strengthened my connection with myself even more.

Most importantly, PSYCH-K® helped me to stop focusing on what I *didn't* want and start focusing on what I *did* want. And that helped me to reconnect with myself: with who I was and what I wanted in my life.

All of the coaching and PSYCH-K® work that I did served to trigger a rebirth of my intuition. My inner voice started to speak up, and for the first time in years, I was able to hear its tiny voice. It was like a whisper, giving me tips on what to do.

Sometimes I listened to it, sometimes I didn't. It's the same today, even though my intuition is even stronger now. It takes a lot of focus to listen to my intuition all the time, and if I don't listen to it and take action right away, my head will step in and speak even louder. I'd been so used to following my head for so many years, it was hard to push it to the back seat and give my intuition the space to take over the driver's seat.

To give you a better idea of what my relationship with my intuition is like these days, I've shared with you how I was able to listen to my intuition and make the decision to write and release this book before two other books that were ahead of it in the schedule. Now I'm going to tell you a little story about how I *didn't* listen to my intuition. Because it isn't always perfect for me in intuition land.

**The video bag**

Once a month I go away to a hotel to work on a business project, on what I call my "workcation weekends." When I was on my way to work on *this particular book* on one of these workcation weekends, I was gathering my things together in my office. I bent down to pick up my computer bag, which was resting next to the video bag that I use when I go out of the office to create videos. It has everything I need to record videos outside of the office, including my tripod and microphone.

As my hand closed around the handles of my computer bag and the video bag caught my eye, my intuition whispered excitedly, "Why don't you grab that bag, too? Then you can do videos while you're away!"

Immediately, my head thundered, "No, don't do that! You're going away to work on your *Business Intuition* book, not to do videos! You don't want to get distracted by videos. You want to write your book. Don't let yourself get distracted! Focus! One thing only!"

And so I left my video bag where it was, in my office. Less than an hour later, I checked into the hotel where I would be staying. It was a new hotel, a place I hadn't stayed before, but it was a nicer chain than the one I usually stayed in. I'm a member of the rewards club for the hotel group that this chain belonged to, and they gave me an upgrade to an even better room than the one I had booked.

The second I walked into my hotel room, I regretted not having brought my video bag. There was a lovely chair with a pretty curtain backdrop that would have made for a nice video set. And the decor was in teal, which is the color of PSYCH-K®! It would have been perfect to do videos for my business. Alas, I listened to my head rather than to my intuition, and I wasn't able to do any new videos in this lovely setting.

The power of these workcation weekends is that I hyperfocus on one thing, and one thing only. Bringing my video bag would have distracted me from writing this book. But it also would have been a nice break from writing to spend an hour or so recording a few videos for my YouTube channel, and I regretted not bringing my video gear.

See what I mean about the power of listening to your intuition? I could have listened to it, but I didn't. My only consolation was to open up the file for my packing list for my workcation weekends, and add to it: "Bring video bag (*even when I don't plan to make videos*)." I hoped that would remind me to bring the bag in the future, and it did: on my following workcation weekend, I brought my video bag and did four quick videos in my room.

The good news was that I learned my lesson. I didn't listen to my intuition the first time around, but I was able to remedy that for a future visit to that hotel.

While the voice of my intuition grows stronger and stronger, and while I pay more attention to it as the days go by, it's still quieter than the voice of my head, or conscious mind. Why? Probably because I've spent the great deal of my life paying more attention to logic and what my head has to say than what my intuition has to say.

I'm still developing my intuition muscle, yet I find that the more I pay attention to my intuition, and take action on what it suggests, the louder its voice becomes. As I review and update this book, I can see that my intuition is much stronger today than it was when I wrote the first edition of it.

~

IF YOU'RE READING this book, I'm going to guess you're in a similar situation. I hope that my story gave you an idea of what it's like to go from being essentially deaf to the voice of intuition to being able to listen to it and to take action on its advice. Let's move on now, and talk a little bit about what exactly I mean by business intuition, why it's so powerful, and how you can develop yours.

# 3

# WHAT IS BUSINESS INTUITION?

*"Intuition is seeing with the soul."*

— DEAN KOONTZ

First of all, what is intuition? It is defined as "the ability to understand something instinctively, without the need for conscious reasoning." It has also been described as "a thing that one knows or considers likely from instinctive feeling rather than conscious reasoning." Business intuition can be defined as business knowledge that one holds based on instinctive feeling rather than conscious reasoning.

**It's also known as:**

- Awareness
- Feeling
- Funny feeling (especially if the intuitive message is perceived as negative)

- Gut feeling
- Heart (though some people also use this term to refer to their emotions, which is different)
- Higher wisdom
- Hunch
- Inner compass
- Inner voice
- Insight
- Instinct
- Little voice
- Perception
- Sixth sense
- Third eye
- True north

I could go on, but I decided to limit the list to some of the more common terms. You may have another word for intuition, and if you do, please continue to use that when you're thinking about it. There's no need to use someone else's terminology if you've got something else that fits better for you.

Intuition is not a conscious process, and it is not a step-by-step procedure using logic, reasoning, or common sense. It's quick, and it usually involves ideas, thoughts, or messages that suddenly pop into your head. Unfortunately, if you haven't trained yourself to grab onto these messages and take action on their advice, they can easily slip away, smothered by the voice of reason, otherwise known as your conscious mind or your head.

**Where does intuition come from?**

We could probably debate this for days, and I'm sure everyone has their own opinion on where intuition originates. I'm going to start with where I think it *doesn't* come from.

If you do a quick online search, you'll find many people claiming that intuition comes from knowledge stored in your subconscious mind. However, in my experience working with the subconscious mind, I have found that unless we've done lots of work to reprogram enhancing beliefs into our subconscious, it's often running on old programs that no longer serve us. These old programs show up in the form of fears and limiting beliefs that keep us stuck safely inside our comfort zone, making it harder for us to take new actions that will help us grow our business.

While our intuition may stem from our unconscious mind, I think it's more likely that it comes from what PSYCH-K® calls the *super*conscious mind, which you may refer to as your higher self, your soul, your spirit, your divine self, or perhaps something else entirely. The super-conscious mind, or higher self, sees the big picture of your life and sends you messages based on your best interest and highest good, and not on what your ego wants.

This is why I (and many others) believe that the wisdom we get from our intuitive messages is so infallible, and why the quote I included earlier from Rachel Wolchin states that "your gut is always right." The way I see it, the messages from our higher selves can't be wrong, and they will always guide you in the right direction. That is, if we interpret them properly, without letting our fears get in the way.

**How does our intuition speak to us?**

Well, it's different for everyone. I mostly get gut feelings, but I also get voices in my head. I know that sounds a little crazy, so please stick with me here. It's the good kind of voices.

I'm a very visual person, and in terms of my learning preferences (visual, auditory, and kinesthetic), I'm visual/kinesthetic. I prefer to learn by reading things, and also by doing them. I'm not very auditory, meaning that I don't *learn* best by listening to things like lectures or podcasts or audiobooks, even though I *enjoy* listening to them.

The information just doesn't stick when I hear it. That's why I make copious notes when I'm learning from a lecture, a podcast, or a video. I write everything down, and that helps me to process the information.

So it doesn't seem logical that my intuition would speak to me with words that I *hear*, but that's actually how it works for me. I also get that gut feeling, which may relate to my kinesthetic learning preference. From my experience, there's not a definite crossover between learning preference and the voice of your intuition.

So if you're a strong auditory learner, your intuition may speak to you differently. Be open to the possibility of receiving messages in whatever way, shape, or form your inner wisdom chooses to send to you. You may be surprised.

I'm going to talk a little bit about the clair senses now. We often hear talk of these in terms of psychic ability, which you may or may not believe in. And if you don't, that's perfectly fine. Belief in psychic ability is absolutely not necessary for you to understand these concepts.

These clair senses are also ways in which our intuition can speak to us, so let's take a look at them. They're like the different "languages" that our intuition uses. You know how we can communicate with each other using the spoken word, the written word, or with sign language? Your intuition also uses verbal, nonverbal, and visual communication.

There are three primary clair senses that you're probably familiar with, and four minor senses that may be new to you. Let's explore these different languages.

## Clairvoyance

When I wrote the first edition of this book, I wrote that I couldn't remember ever experiencing this, despite being a highly visual person. But since then, I've realized that I'm getting more and more messages in this way. For the past few months, I've been getting images of places popping into my head, and I get the sense that these are places that I need to return to—either to write about them, or simply to visit. These images are usually accompanied by a sense of longing to return there. My gut says that it's more than just a desire to go on holiday; there's something more to be experienced in this locations.

This particular "language" or method of communication involves presenting you with visual cues or symbols. You might get a specific mental image that will give you clues as to what your intuition is trying to tell you. They may come to you during meditation, or they may pop into your head during the day, as you're doing something else. They may be accompanied by a gut feeling that tells you what you need to know about this image or symbol, or they may simply appear on their own.

## Clairaudience

This is one of the main languages my intuition uses to speak to me. I'll hear words, either single words or phrases, that pop up in my mind. Often I'll get these messages during a quiet moment when I'm in between tasks. They also can come when I'm doing some kind of repetitive exercise, like running or walking, where I can quickly get into the zone, a mental state where I'm relaxed and not thinking about anything in particular.

Have you ever heard of "shower thoughts?" Shower thoughts refer to any idea you might have while carrying out a routine task like showering, driving, or daydreaming. Sometimes they're random, silly connections that your brain makes (I'm thinking of the subreddit /r/shower-thoughts on the Reddit.com website, which you might find entertaining), but often they're useful bits of inner wisdom. If you're the kind of person who gets regular shower thoughts, you might want to keep a pen and paper in the bathroom to record your ideas once you get out of the water.

## Clairsentience

This is another one of the languages my intuition uses to speak to me. I get a gut feeling about something. It could be a message that something is right or wrong for me, or that I should or should not do something. Or I could get a feeling when I see a particular object or person that makes me stop and pause, allowing more information to come to me via clairaudience. Some people describe this as a feeling of expansion (yes, good, right) or contraction (no, bad, not right).

This communication method involves getting a feeling somewhere in your body, without any outer stimuli to trigger that feeling. It could be in your gut, or it could involve chills all over your body. Have you ever gotten goosebumps when someone said something that resonated with you? This is your inner wisdom's way of saying, "Hey! Pay attention."

## Clairempathy

This may relate to clairsentience, or that gut feeling that I get. I usually get very, very strong first impressions of people, and they're *always* right. Whenever I've allowed my head to override that first impression, it always leads to trouble.

Clairempathy allows us to sense or feel the attitudes, emotions, or beliefs of another person. It's like you feel their energy or vibration, and that can give you useful information about that person. This could be your intuition's way of giving you valuable details that your conscious mind might not pick up.

## Clairgustance

This is an odd one: it involves tasting a substance or food without having anything in your mouth. Because this is such a strange sensation, it may simply be your intuition telling you to pay attention, or it may be a way of providing some type of (tasty) symbol that directly relates to the message you need to receive. It might also be a way of letting you know whether something is right (delicious) or wrong (not delicious) for you. This is purely speculation because I've never experienced this sensation.

## Clairscent

This is precisely what it sounds like: smelling a fragrance or an odor that is not present in your surroundings. I've experienced this before, for example, smelling a familiar perfume that someone I knew wears, despite them not being present, but I've never been able to relate it to a particular message. Again, this may be another way of your intuition getting your attention or sending you a direct message. It might also be a way of letting you know whether something is right (appealing scent) or wrong (unappealing scent) for you.

I once went through an extended period of time where I would randomly smell something burning—when in fact there was nothing on fire. I always had the sensation that something was trying to get my attention, and perhaps it was simply my intuition saying, "Hey!" Unfortunately, I could never figure out what it was that I was meant to pay attention to. This phenomenon happened for months, possibly years, but it no longer occurs. Perhaps my system realized that it wasn't serving its purpose because I wasn't picking up on the meaning of the signal.

## Clairtangency

In psychic terms, this usually refers to someone who can handle an object or touch something and receive information about that object. In terms of intuition, this could mean touching a thing and receiving some type of message from your intuition, either about that object or about something completely unrelated. The object might serve as a trigger for your intuition to speak to you, giving you a much clearer message via clairvoyance, clairaudience, or clairsentience.

## Take Action Today

As you read through the different clair senses, which ones sounded familiar? Which of the senses have you experienced in your own life? Write this down in your journal, along with some times when you've experienced your intuition speaking to you in these ways.

## On the podcast

Below is a list of related podcast episodes. I've been producing a weekly podcast since 2013, and it's full of useful resources that will help support you on your journey to visibility and personal growth. Most episodes now have downloadable transcripts, so you can read as you listen, or instead of listening.

You can find the full list of podcast episodes here: www.hollyworton.com/podcast

- 292 Joanna Hennon + Holly ~ What's Better: Spirit Guides or Tapping into Your Intuition? Part II (now with downloadable transcript!)
- 290 Jo Casey + Holly ~ What's Better: Spirit Guides or Tapping into Your Intuition? (now with downloadable transcript!)
- 235 Joanna Hennon + Holly ~ How to Find the Right Balance Between Structure and Intuition (now with downloadable transcript!)
- 162 Tap Into Your Intuition to Make Your Business Easier
- 141 Caroline Frenette ~ How to Master Your Intuition to Create Quantum Leaps in Business
- 83 How to Follow Your Creative Intuition, with Flora Bowley
- 79 How to Tap Into Your Intuition & Add Magic to Your Business, with Fifi Mills

## 4

# WHEN WE IGNORE BUSINESS INTUITION

*"I feel there are two people inside me -- me and my intuition. If I go against her, she'll screw me every time, and if I follow her, we get along quite nicely."*

— Kim Basinger

You're probably already familiar with what it looks like to have an *underdeveloped* sense of business intuition. When we're not in alignment with our intuition, or not listening to it, or we're hearing the messages but not taking action, business can be difficult. If we're not focused on our inner guidance, then we're probably focused on seeking advice from outside ourselves.

This is not always a bad thing: seeing a business coach or mentor can be a really powerful experience, especially when that person is really aligned with you and your business. My business coach/mentor, Lisa Wechtenhiser (http://lisamw.com), calls herself "practically woo" because, in addition to providing practical business advice, she also channels her clients' guides during a session, bringing a new dimension to business mentoring. The sessions I've had with Lisa have been the most aligned, resonant business mentoring sessions I've ever had.

I trust everything she and my guides tell me to do, and I easily take action on those things. My work with Lisa has helped me to stop playing small and step up in a much bigger way with my business. The advice I get just feels right for me.

But there's another kind of business mentoring, where business gurus offer up a cookie cutter approach to entrepreneurship, assuring you that if their method worked for them, then it can work for you, too. And it can. The problem, however, is that their approach may or may not be the *best* strategy for you. And while their method may technically work, if it feels out of alignment, you may come across a bit "off" when using it in your business. And that energy can be off-putting to potential clients.

In between these two approaches lies a whole gamut of business coaching and mentoring: professionals who have the best intentions for you and your business, but still aren't quite the right fit for you. And that's when you can get off track by following their advice.

I won't tell you every single story of every situation where I got off track by following other people's business advice, but I think it might be useful for you to hear a few examples so you know that you're not alone.

### The mentoring program

A friend of mine got amazing results from working with a particular business mentor, and when this mentor opened up a new group mentoring program, I was tempted to work with her. She was a master at sales, and her offer was so compelling that I felt like I couldn't say no. I saw her speak at an event, and was so tempted to sign up, but for some reason wasn't fully convinced.

I saw her speak a week later at another event, and I was still going back and forth on whether or not to sign up. I spoke with my friend about it, and with my husband, and I was completely torn. It was a big investment, and I'd have to use savings to pay for it. It's hard for me to express just how much indecision I felt; suffice to say that every hour or so I went back and forth between wanting to sign up and deciding not to do it. The program had been the catalyst to jump start my friend's business, which made it seem like such a great thing. But there was something that just wasn't quite right, and I had no clue what that was.

In the end, I signed up for the program. The trainings were pretty basic, mostly things I already knew about operating a small business. The mentoring calls weren't what I'd call life-changing, and I didn't get much out of them, either. In the end, I simply didn't get great results out of the program, and I was disappointed with myself for having succumbed to a fancy sales pitch.

It wasn't until a couple of years later, after my business evolved from social media marketing into business mindset work, that I fully understood what had happened. At the time, I wasn't yet running the business that I was meant to be running, and I wasn't fully passionate about the work that I was doing, though I hadn't realized it at the time.

My intuition knew this, and it knew that it wasn't the right mentoring program for me, and it wasn't the right time for me to make such a big investment. It was a waste of time and money for me, even though it was clearly an excellent program for other people. I had made the wrong decision by listening to my head, rather than following my intuition.

### The big name coach

Some time after this, I signed up to a coaching program with an online coach I greatly admired. I had investigated the different ways of working with her, and after going back and forth on what to do, I decided to sign up to her biggest package. I wanted big results!

You'd think I would have learned after my previous mistake, but I hadn't. I knew this person, and I knew her background. Because I had trained as a coach a few years before, I knew what coaching was, and I knew what I wanted and needed: coaching. I needed clarity, and I needed accountability.

This person, however, had not trained as a coach. She simply had lots of experience building a successful business, and was now passing on that knowledge to others. What she was offering was more along the lines of mentoring than coaching. And mentoring was not what I wanted or needed at that time.

The sessions started, and I was so confused. They weren't what I was expecting. There was no accountability, no helping me to dig deep and get clarity. She was giving out a lot of advice based on her experience, and a lot of it just wasn't resonating with me.

Once again, I was so disappointed. I had wasted time and money once more, and I wasn't getting the results I had hoped for. It wasn't until the final session, where I came with a list of questions and essentially picked her brain for the entire hour, that I felt like I got a lot of value from the call. It had taken the entire package for me to understand what she could actually offer, and unfortunately, it wasn't what I had initially needed or wanted.

Again, I was still in the middle of my social media business at the time, so it wasn't yet the right time for me to invest in something like this. I had let my head dictate the decision, rather than going with my intuition, which had tried to help me by making me debate back and forth about signing up for a couple of months before actually doing it. Sadly, in the end I listened to my head and not my gut. Wrong move!

## The online programs

I've enrolled in numerous online programs over the years, despite the fact that I'm fully aware that this is *not* my preferred method of learning. I hate signing up to a course that's dished out in small portions over the course of several weeks. I want to learn *just* what I need to learn, *when* I need to learn it. I don't want extra information cluttering up my mind, and I don't want to have to wait until Week 4 to learn what I really need.

I prefer learning through *reading*, where I can skim ahead to see the bits that I want to focus on. Also, I learn best through the written word, rather than the spoken word. But of course the online business world knows that many people value multimedia courses and video over books, so that's what most people offer.

I digress. There are many online programs that come to mind when writing this. The important thing to share is that it can be so tempting to sign up to a program that has such carefully crafted sales copy that it seems to speak *directly to us*. You know what I'm talking about, don't you?

And despite the fact that my intuition has warned me against signing up for many an online program, I've gone ahead and done it anyway. I've gotten so bogged down with live calls, recorded videos, guided meditations, worksheets, and Facebook groups, that in the end I've become overwhelmed by all the information that ended up being 90% not what I needed and only 10% useful to me.

It's happened so many times, that I finally learned from it. I recently received an email from an entrepreneur offering a new online course on a topic that I wanted to learn more about, and I emailed her to ask what level it was intended for and how long it would take to get through all the videos. Once she assured me that they were quite short, I blocked out two days in my calendar: one to watch the entire course, and one to implement what I'd learned. It was perfect. There was still a lot of information in there that I already knew, but it was useful, and it didn't take up too much of my time.

### What about you?

When have you ignored your business intuition? What mistakes or wrong turns have you made by not following your gut feeling? How has that impacted your business and life? What can you learn from it?

# 5

# WHEN WE LISTEN TO BUSINESS INTUITION

*"Intuition is always right in at least two important ways: It is always in response to something. It always has your best interest at heart."*

— GAVIN DE BECKER

You may or not be familiar with what it looks like to have a well developed sense of business intuition. Since you're reading this book, I'm going to guess that you don't. When we are in alignment with our intuition, and listen to it, and we hear the messages and take action on them, business can be easy. If we're focused on our inner guidance, then we're probably experiencing a business that flows easily and feels effortless.

As I mentioned earlier, this can take time to develop, but it's like a muscle. The more we pay attention to our intuition, the easier it is to hear the little voice. It's like having our own personal business mentor inside of ourselves. This doesn't mean that we no longer benefit from working with an external business coach or mentor, it just means that we've got a very powerful source of infallible advice within ourselves.

As before, I won't tell you every single story of every situation where I got my business in flow by following my business intuition, but I think it might be useful for you to hear a few examples so you know what it's like to listen to that inner voice.

## The big move

When I was deep in my business sabbatical, I took a trip to Italy to see my spiritual teacher. During the week of his birthday, which falls during the summer, people come from all over the world to get together in the coastal town where he lives. It's a great time for personal development: many of the people in our group are holistic therapists and offer sessions, and there's often a wellness week that's offered, with all kinds of holistic wellbeing classes.

I had traveled alone to Italy, and my intuition delivered a big message when I was at the airport in Rome on my way home. As always, it was a rough transition back to the "real world," after being surrounded by so many like-minded people from my spiritual group. The airport was busy, flights were delayed, and I was tired.

I was waiting in line to check in for my flight, and there was a very annoying woman in front of me, yelling at the airline workers and complaining about something. She was being very high difficult and very disrespectful, and I just wanted her to be quiet and go away. I could tell from her accent that she was from Argentina, which is where I was living at the time and where I was returning to.

Suddenly, it struck me that I had no desire whatsoever to return to Argentina. I missed my partner (now husband), and I was looking forward to seeing him, but that was all. I was tired of my life there, and I was ready for something new. We had discussed moving to Europe at some time in the future, and my intuition was telling me that this was the time.

When I returned home, I shared my idea, and we instantly began making plans to move to Europe. We decided on England as our destination, and we've lived there ever since. It was thanks to this move that I embarked on my journey to becoming a coach, and I was able to create the business that I have today.

## The business transitions

After training as a coach, I started out by setting up a life coaching business. I really struggled to get things started, so I ended up deciding to merge my coaching skills with my experience in online marketing and help people learn how to use social media to market themselves. I went through a few niche ideas until I settled on working with authors. I ran this business for some time, before my intuition spoke up and gave me an idea.

I had run the first iteration of my online program, and only one of the attendees had been an author. The others were all holistic therapists, and because of my coaching background and my previous experience running a holistic spa as part of my first company, I really enjoyed working with them.

I was listening to a lot of guided meditations at that time, particularly the ones by my friend Cara Wilde (http://carawilde.com). One night, as I was about to fall asleep after listening to a guided journey, my intuition whispered, "Why don't you change your business to work with holistic therapists, rather than authors?"

My head replied, "No way! You've changed your business so many times now that no one will ever take you seriously. Stick with what you've got."

But the idea stuck with me. I remembered it first thing after waking up the following morning, and the idea niggled at my mind for days. I went back and forth, worrying that no one would ever take me seriously if I changed my business niche once again. Finally, I gave into my intuition and changed my business niche. The second I made that decision, it felt right in my gut.

Eventually even that business niche didn't feel right, and I changed once again, focusing on the mindset work that I did when I wrote the first edition of this book. Once again, I took up my old coaching brand, Ready to Bloom, which I had always loved. I built my mindset business around that brand for over a year, until my intuition spoke up once more, whispering: "That's not right for you anymore. Use your own name."

My head admonished me: "You can't rebrand yet again. It's too soon. Don't be unprofessional and flaky. Stick with what you've got."

But I followed my intuition's advice, and rebranded my business mindset company using my own name. As soon as I did, I felt as though I had been hiding behind business names for the past few years, and was now able to step fully into my vision for myself and my business. It just felt right.

**The business books**

I've loved writing ever since I was a child, and wrote my first books at the age of seven. I grew up and quit writing, but I still loved reading and in the back of my mind wished I were a writer. But I had grown busy with other things, and now I understand that it just wasn't the right time.

Through my Tribal Publishing company, where I

helped authors learn to use social media, I learned a lot about self publishing and marketing books. I learned from traditionally published authors that the big publishers didn't do much marketing for new authors, and only really invested in the big name writers. I learned just how easy it was to self publish an ebook, a print on demand paperback, and create an audiobook. I learned all the steps of a self publishing book project.

Earlier in 2016, my intuition whispered, "It's time. Write a book." I had started writing a life coaching book years before, and had never finished it. I had ideas for how to transform that book into a business book, and that was my first instinct of where to start.

Around the same time, I got the idea for writing a book of business belief statements, the kind of enhancing—or positive—belief statements that I use with my clients. My original idea was to create a pdf ebook that people could download from my website. But my intuition had a better idea, and whispered to me: "Why don't you create a Kindle ebook instead?"

And that's how my first book, *Business Beliefs: 600+ Beliefs That Make Up a Successful Business Mindset*, was born. I was so excited by how easy the process was that my intuition delivered several other book ideas, and I wrote them down in my business notebook, where I store all my ideas. I had so many book ideas that I decided to write and release one book each month for the rest of the year, and I grew excited by the prospect of releasing so many books.

But my head said, "How can you do that? No one will take you seriously if you release so many books. You should do less. No one writes a book a month."

Fortunately I ignored my head, and continued on my plan to release one book each month. It feels right, and it's exciting to have a new creation to launch every few weeks.

It's helped my business by getting me out there and making me more visible with what I do, and it's helped me to stretch outside of my comfort zone.

I later saw other people doing the same, and it further confirmed my belief that I had done the right thing. Michelle Kulp, a book launch expert who helped me with the launch of one of my books, recently wrote a book called *28 Books to $100K: A Guide for Ambitious Authors Who Want to Skyrocket Their Passive Income By Writing a Book a Month.* Not long after, she released a fantastic online course (yes, I bought it—and I love it) with the same name.

## The big pivot

Eventually, in late 2018, I decided that I loved writing so much that I wanted to quit business mindset coaching and dedicate myself to writing as much as I could. But that was another tough decision. My gut was telling me that I needed to quit coaching, but my head was afraid.

I was afraid that people wouldn't take me seriously. I was so fickle! Pivoting my business once again? I was afraid I'd look like one of those people who picks a niche, works on it for a couple of months, then changes their mind over and over before ever establishing themselves in any kind of business.

But my gut is smarter than my head, so I listened to it. I spent much of the following year writing, and I published *If Trees Could Talk*, a book that was totally unrelated to anything I had ever written before. More than a pivot, this was a giant leap into something new.

In 2020, once again, I published a book a month, and I hope to do the same in 2021. Writing is what I love most. It makes my heart sing, and it's a way for me to help more people than I could with one-to-one coaching. Despite all of the challenges that 2020 has presented, it's been a mostly joy-filled year—and I'm positive it's because I've spent so much time writing.

**What about you?**

When have you listened to your business intuition and followed its advice? How have you experienced synchronicity or "good luck" by following your gut feeling? How has that impacted your business and life? What can you learn from it?

# 6

# THE POWER OF BUSINESS INTUITION

*"Don't let the noise of others' opinions drown out your own inner voice. And most important, have the courage to follow your heart and intuition."*

— STEVE JOBS

I hope that my stories have helped show you the power of being in listening to and taking action on our business intuition. If you've read my first two business mindset books in this series, *Business Beliefs* and *Business Blocks*, you'll be familiar with my 15 categories of business beliefs and blocks. I'd like to revisit those to share with you some examples of the power of business intuition.

## Action and Goals

Being in touch with our intuition can help us to take actions that our head might otherwise veto. It can help us to stretch outside of our comfort zone and do things that we're afraid of. It can help us to set bigger goals for ourselves.

When I set the goal to write a book a month, my head got in the way. But my gut knew that it was the right path forward. It was a big goal that stretched me, but now that I've done it, I know that I can repeat the process another year. This will help me increase my income streams and generate more revenue for my business.

## Change and Growth

Change can be scary, let's face it. But when a decision to change or pivot comes from the gut rather than the head, it can make things easier. The mind can get in the way, bombarding us with fears and limiting beliefs. But the gut knows better.

If I hadn't listened to my gut all those times it was telling me to pivot—even when my head was screaming not to—I wouldn't be where I am today. I'd be doing something else, something that my head perceived as safer. And I probably wouldn't be as happy.

## Clients and Boundaries

How many times have you taken on a client when you knew that they weren't a good fit? Hopefully, that hasn't happened too often, but I think we've all been there, especially in the early stages of business. Thankfully, I learned to trust my gut and not take on every client who wanted to work with me.

Oftentimes, when I had a discovery call with a potential client, I would get a strong gut feeling for whether or not they were a good fit for me. When they weren't, I would refer them to someone else or suggest they do the

PSYCH-K® training themselves so they could do the work on their own. (To be fair, I often recommended this training to all kinds of people, even those I enjoyed working with, because it's such a valuable technique to have).

## Confidence & Trust

It can boost your confidence in your innate wisdom, because you'll have an increasingly strong sense of inner knowing. You'll never have to rely on someone else's advice ever again...unless you want to. I still work with healers, coaches, and mentors to improve my mindset and my business. I still learn from others.

But I always come back to my intuition when making decisions for my business—big and small. This has increased my self-confidence and self-trust, and it feels incredibly powerful. Making decisions has never been so easy, simply because I trust myself.

## Creativity

Listening to your intuition can boost your imagination and creativity by allowing you to have a steady flow of creative ideas that will help improve your business. Ideas will just pop into your head, and you'll never be wondering what to do next in your business.

I keep files in Evernote for all my creative ideas. Whenever something pops into my head, I put it into the file for podcast episode topics, or book ideas, or blog posts. When it's time to record a new podcast episode, or write a new blog post, I have a list of topics to choose from. And when I'm ready to start a new book project, I can just pick one and start writing. These are all ideas that have come to my through listening to my intuition. It just makes content creation easier.

## Leadership and Outsourcing

It can make you more sensitive to the energy of the people around you, giving you a clear "first impression" of them that will help you to understand how you feel about them, making it clear whether or not they're the right person for you to do joint ventures or make other business plans with.

Listening to your intuition can help you to hire the right people, whether it's employees or freelancers. It can help you to build the perfect team for your business. Your intuition can also help you to let go of people when they're just not right. Firing people is hard, and often our head can get in the way, telling us: "Oh, they'll get better. They'll improve soon." When all the time our gut knows that they're not the right person for the role.

When I ran my first company with my business partner, there were far too many times that we hired the wrong people just because we needed to fill the role and there weren't any suitable candidates. As you can imagine, this never worked out well. My gut always knew the person wasn't right, but my head would always say "Well, there's no one else, is there?"

When I hired my podcast editor back in 2013, I just knew in my gut that he was the right person. Now, seven years later, he's still working for me, and I've recommended him to many other business owners (if you want his details, just get in touch).

## Learning

Listening to our intuition can help us make better choices about how to learn all the things we need to learn to run our business effectively. It can help us to say no to the mentor with the fancy sales pitch and say yes to one who just *feels* right. Our intuition can also help us to choose a good business book over the high-ticket online course, if we know deep down that reading is our preferred method of learning, and not video.

I'm now very, very picky about how I choose to learn. I continue to learn primarily through books, but I do sign up for the occasional online course. I'm also learning which online business owners are good at creating streamlined courses that are light on fluff, and which ones sell courses that are filled with padding.

I recently took an online course on iPhone photography, because I wanted to improve my pictures for my blog. I learned a lot, but I never finished the course because it was filled with so much fluff. And when the creator of the course sent out an email to entice me to sign up for the photography *editing* course, I was tempted (because I wanted to learn that information) but I held out because I didn't want another time-wasting course.

## Lifestyle

There's no sense in running a business that doesn't fit into our ideal lifestyle. Yes, sometimes we need to do things we don't want to do, but if we get caught up in running a business the way others think we should rather than the way is best for us, it can lead to unnecessary stress and burnout.

I got to the point where I no longer wanted to run one-to-one sessions. I wanted to write books! My head wasn't crazy about the idea, but my gut knew it was the right fit for the flexible and free lifestyle that I want for myself. Now that I'm no longer working to fill my calendar with discovery calls and client calls, I feel much more relaxed and less stressed about my weeks.

## Marketing & Sales

Listening to your gut means that you won't follow sales and marketing techniques that don't feel right to you. Yes, sometimes we need to step outside of our comfort zone when engaging in marketing and sales, and sometimes that feels uncomfortable. But it's a very different kind of uncomfortable when something just isn't right for you.

This means that if you hate doing videos, you can find other ways of marketing your business. You can podcast or write blog posts. If you hate cold calling, you can do something else instead. You can spread the word about your business in the way that works for you.

## Money

Money is a tricky thing, and for many of us this is the most important aspect of our business mindset to work on. Listening to our intuition can help us to make better decisions in all areas of business, which can increase turnover and profit.

This year, when I was working hard to write my twelve books in twelve months, someone suggested to me that a good income stream would be to offer one-to-one client sessions again. It was tempting: a one-to-one session is a much bigger price than one of my books. But I knew how stressed I got with having client calls in the calendar, and my intuition said "No, NO, NO!" And so I didn't.

**Personal Power**

Personal power is made up of the layers of self-trust, self-love, self-acceptance, self-esteem, self-confidence, self-value, and self-worth. Improving our intuition can help with increasing all of these things. Listening to your gut rather than to the opinions of others is incredibly empowering.

I used to make elaborate pro/con lists in order to make even the simplest decisions. Now, I feel the power of my intuition and I make quick decisions. I trust myself, I know myself, and I know my strengths. It feels powerful. And this is all thanks to trusting my intuition.

**Strategy, Clarity and Vision**

When we ignore our intuition, we make bad investments in our business, we give away our power to others by always looking outside ourselves for answers, and we don't trust the decisions we make. This can lead to us feeling stuck and frustrated with our business.

However, when we follow our business intuition, it's like having an inner compass or GPS system that directs our thoughts and actions. It gives us useful bits of advice, and it helps us quickly and easily make decisions by giving us us crystal clarity of mind, which takes the stress out of knowing which path to choose for our business. Our intuition helps us to simply *know* if an opportunity is good or not, and easily take decisive action when it is.

It helps us to instinctively know which projects and actions are high priority, so we know what to focus on, and it aids us in focusing with laser clarity so we can get those tasks done more quickly and easily because we're confident that they're the right things for us to be doing at that time.

This takes the stress out of working through our to do list, because we instinctively know which actions to start working on, meaning that we get these done easily, we manage our time better, and we feel satisfied at the end of our day.

When we intuitively know that we're on the right path, making the right decisions and focusing on the highest priority actions, it gives us peace of mind and makes it easier for us to have fun with our business. Things are less stressful, because we have the confidence to say no to the opportunities that aren't right for us, meaning that we have more time to focus on the things that will take us down the best path for our business.

It can help you to clearly understand problems that arise, which makes it easier for you to solve them. In the same way, it also makes decisions quick and easy, because you'll always know exactly what to do. No more agonizing over decisions and making pro/con lists...unless you want to.

You'll always know how to work around any challenges that come up, which can make your life and business feel easy and effortless because you'll have the confidence in your ability to work through anything.

**Success and Opportunities**

When we trust our intuition, we're more likely to take actions outside of our comfort zone. We're less likely to be blocked by fears and limiting beliefs. This means that we're more likely to say yes to opportunities outside of our comfort zone, which can lead to increased success.

In 2019, I hired a public relations expert who specialized in books and authors. She got me a spot on national television in the UK, and when she first contacted me to confirm that I was okay with the appearance, I wanted to say no. My head was full of fears. But my gut said yes, and I'm so pleased that I grabbed that opportunity, because it led to many other media appearances.

**Value and Self-Worth**

Trusting your intuition can help you to increase your self-worth and know your value. By consistently making better decisions, it can help us to improve our business and really know our value and worth.

When I was doing one-to-one client sessions, there was a time when I priced my sessions higher than one of my instructors. This felt wrong. But I knew that my clients were getting big results in their businesses after working with me (to the tune of tens of thousands of dollars), and my gut said that I needed to price my sessions accordingly, even though my head thought it was wrong.

**Visibility**

Fears, blocks, and limiting beliefs can mean that our head says "NO!" to new opportunities for marketing and sales. They can keep us playing small in business. But when we listen to our gut, this can help to override a negative mindset and help us to say yes to new things, which can increase our visibility and get us known to our ideal clients.

As I shared earlier, saying yes to my gut led to first one, then further appearances on national television. This boosted my visibility and got my books known in the world, leading to increased sales. All thanks to my intuition.

. . .

DOESN'T THAT SOUND FANTASTIC? It is. I know what it's like to be totally disconnected from my inner wisdom and I know what it's like to feel that deeper connection with myself that makes business and life so much easier. I want this for you.

# 7

# DEVELOPING YOUR BUSINESS INTUITION

*"Insight is not a lightbulb that goes off inside our heads. It is a flickering candle that can easily be snuffed out."*

— MALCOLM GLADWELL

I f you're feeling totally out of touch with yourself and your intuition, like I was, it may seem like your intuition is completely silent. Trust me, it's there, like the lightly glowing embers of a fire that's almost gone out. You just need to rekindle the flame and help it to grow. Let's explore how you can do that.

## Step 1: Make space

The first step in developing your intuition is to make space by decluttering your mind. It's hard to listen to the tiny whisper of your intuition when your mind is cluttered with stuff. There are many ways to do this, and you can try one or all of the suggestions below. I find that it makes it much,

much easier to listen to my intuition when my mind is free of clutter.

It's like when we have to wait patiently on the platform for people to get off the subway or train before we get on. Otherwise, if people try to go in and out at the same time, it's chaos. Allow yourself to declutter first, which will make space for the intuitive messages to come in.

## Mind Decluttering Meditation

I often recommend what I call my Mind Decluttering Meditation. I first developed this when I joined my spiritual group years ago, and found that my mind was so busy it was difficult to concentrate on the simple seventeen minute exercise that I needed to do each day. Each morning when I sat down to do my exercise, which is a bit like meditation, all kinds of thoughts rushed through my mind.

I eventually noticed that most of them had to do with things on my to do list, or tasks that I hadn't yet put on my list, or actions that I was afraid of forgetting. I had recently read David Allen's book *Getting Things Done*, and I fully understood the importance of getting tasks out of my head and into my system for getting them done. I decided to do a little pre-exercise "meditation" to declutter my mind.

Here's how you do it: sit down in a quiet place, as if you were to meditate. Keep a piece of paper, notebook, or computer by your side where you can make note of things that come up. Close your eyes, and relax as if you were going to meditate. The second something pops into your mind, don't try to release it. Open your eyes, and make note of it. Then go back to your "meditation." Keep recording your thoughts, ideas, and tasks until your mind is clear, or for as much time as you've allotted for this activity.

You may wish to continue this mind decluttering "meditation" every day for several days, or until you feel like you've gotten everything out of your head and into your system for getting things done. After that, you may wish to do the meditation from time to time, or once a week, or whenever you feel that the voice of your intuition has quieted down.

## Release mind chatter

Our minds are often filled with negative mind chatter that goes beyond the clutter of our to do list. The way I release negative mind chatter with myself—and how I used to work with clients—is by using PSYCH-K® to reinforce positive beliefs, thus releasing the limiting beliefs that make up our unwanted mind gremlins. PSYCH-K® can also be used to release fears, stress, and past traumas.

I use PSYCH-K® because that's what works best for me, but if you want to let go of your mind gremlins, then it's important that you find the technique that works best for *you*. That could be PSYCH-K®, or it could be NLP, EFT, TAT, hypnotherapy, or something else. You might need to try a few different techniques before you find what works for you.

Not only do I do the work with myself, but I occasionally hire other professionals to help me with things that I can't manage to shift on my own. No matter how much experience I have with mindset work, there are always things that I can't see clearly, simply because I'm in my head all day long. By seeing another professional, I can get to the root of some things much faster.

## Give yourself permission

It can be scary to give ourselves permission to focus on something that may be considered "woo woo" by our culture. But how you decide to run your company and how you make your decisions are no one's business but your own—literally—and if your gut is telling you that it's time to start paying attention to your intuition, then it's time to give yourself permission to do just that.

Giving yourself permission is as simple as that. If you're reading this book, I'm going to assume that you're an adult. As children, we have to get permission from for just about everything—to go play at a friend's house, to speak up in class, to go to the bathroom at school—and as adults we sometimes fall into the trap of waiting for some nonexistent authority figure to give us permission to do the things that we want to do, when in reality that's not necessary at all.

Recognize that you have the authority to give yourself permission to do things. Understand that developing to your intuition is important to you, and make the conscious decision that it's okay for you to do so. That's all you need to do -- make a conscious decision to give yourself permission to cultivate your intuition. It's okay.

If you use PSYCH-K® or other processes to reprogram your subconscious mind, you might want to create a belief statement such as 'I give myself permission to listen to the wisdom of my intuition and take action on its advice" and then program that into your subconscious.

## Release your resistance

You may have some resistance to fully tuning into your meditation, and that's perfectly natural. Many of us place much more value on logical reasoning, because Western culture values it so much, and going against the grain may feel uncomfortable because it's outside of our comfort zone.

Release your resistance by accepting the messages that come when you get an intuitive hunch or gut feeling—don't call yourself crazy. Accept whatever you see, hear, or feel, even if it doesn't make sense at the time. Recognize that it's your intuition speaking, and understand that if you're really out of touch with yourself, it might be an unfamiliar voice. Be accepting of what comes.

If you use PSYCH-K® or other techniques to reprogram your subconscious mind, you might want to create a belief statement such as "I easily receive the messages from my intuition and take action on them" and then program that into your subconscious.

### Physically declutter or clean

Physically decluttering or cleaning your home and office may also help to declutter your mind. Go through your home room by room, rounding up the things that no longer serve you, and either take them to a charity shop, recycle them, or throw them away. Money mindset mentor Denise Duffield-Thomas has a fabulous list of 38 Things You Need to Declutter From Your Life NOW that might help get you motivated to physically declutter your life.

Because we're focusing on business intuition here, it's especially important to go through your office and declutter. Here's what to declutter in your office:

**Receipts of business expenses.** Hopefully you've got a system for this. I have a 12-pocket accordion folder that I stuff them all into, organized according to each month, but I don't do it every day or even every week, and they tend to pile up in a drawer. Grab all your business expense receipts and put them into your system, whatever that may be.

**Stuff you've printed.** Have you printed out articles to read, emails, or anything else? Go through this all and see if you really need the hard copy. If not, get rid of it. Be sure you still have the original files of the documents before throwing them away, or scan the printouts to get them back into digital form if you can't find the original files.

**Notes you've taken.** I have notebooks that I use for taking notes, but occasionally I handwrite things on separate pieces of paper. Get these into whatever system you need: are they things to do, notes from a coaching session, or something else? Put them where they belong, or scan them so you've got them on your computer.

**Old client files.** After I stopped doing one-to-one client work, I burned my old client files. It would have taken ages to shred them, so I just made a bonfire in the barbecue. It felt very symbolic, a literal burning down the bridge between my old work and my current work.

**Handwritten to-do lists.** I also have a system for this, but I do tend to jot things down on little pieces of paper and then leave them all over my desk. Get these into your to-do system, which hopefully is digital, so you can eliminate the paper.

**Those little slips of paper.** In addition to writing things to do on those little pieces of paper, I make all kinds of notes. Get rid of them! Put the information wherever it needs to be, and then get rid of the paper.

**Any other papers.** Get rid of everything you can. If there's a digital copy of it, then toss the printout. If there's no digital copy, scan it and save it on your computer. It's that simple. You'll find that there are actually very few pieces of paper that you'll actually need around to refer to on a daily basis.

**Old digital files.** Go through your files and folders on your computer, and delete (or move to an external hard drive or cloud drive) anything that you no longer need. Delete duplicate files, old photographs, everything that takes up space on your computer.

**Old hard drives.** Just because they're not on your computer doesn't mean that they're not taking up space. Get rid of stuff you don't need on old hard drives.

**Old emails.** I once went through my Gmail account and deleted every single email before a particular date. It felt very freeing to get rid of old correspondence, and some of it was so old that I knew I'd never need it.

**Old books.** Go through your bookshelves. Are there any books you're keeping that you never intend to read again? Purge: take them to a charity shop, leave them at your local train station, release them into the wild using BookCrossing, or give them away to friends. Clear up your bookshelves by getting rid of unwanted books and tidy them up. I have very deep bookshelves in my office, and sometimes I use the space in front of the books to lay things on. Clean this up!

Go through your desk and declutter all surfaces, then go through each and every drawer and get rid of everything you don't use or no longer need. Take it to a charity shop, recycle it, or throw it away. Purge, purge, purge.

You get the idea: declutter your office. It can give you peace of mind and the space to let those intuitive messages come through more smoothly.

∾

## Step 2: Tune in

Now that you've made space by decluttering your mind, there are so many ways you can tune into receiving messages from your intuition. It's all about getting your mind in the right place so that you can hear the messages. Think of it as tuning into the right channel on the radio: there's a lot of static in between stations, but when you find the right frequency, a station will come in clearly. There are many ways to do this, and you can try one or all of the suggestions below.

### Meditate

This is probably one of the most commonly recommended ways of accessing our meditation, so I'm including this first, even though I rarely do it myself. Messages from our intuition tend to be easier to hear when we're in a quiet space, so spending time alone, in silence, will help you to hear these messages when they pop up.

One thing that I do, however, is to take a break about halfway through my workday to have a "moment." I listen to some meditation-style music on my phone, and I lie down on my bed to rest. I'll do this for 15-20 minutes, and it helps me to rest, regenerate, and get ready for the second half of my work day. It's also a time when all kinds of things pop into my head, which I can write down. Sometimes it's to-do clutter, and sometimes it's valuable ideas.

### Try guided visualizations

This is one of the ways I first started getting messages from my intuition. I downloaded some guided meditations from Cara Wilde's old website, WildBliss.com, and listened to them every night before going to bed. Some of them, such as the one titled Creating Emotional Balance, are intended to help you get clarity on a situation. Awakening Your Dream Self helps you to call out your deepest desires and heart-felt dreams, which then allows the universe to send you new opportunities and signposts in your day-to-day reality. Hm...sounds a bit like intuition, doesn't it?

You can use whatever guided meditations you feel drawn to. Find someone whose voice is relaxing and sooth-ing, and make space in your day or night to listen to them. I prefer to listen to them before falling asleep, but you may prefer to listen in the evenings or whenever you have a quiet moment throughout the day. Do what works for you.

**Go on a nature walk**

If you follow me on Instagram (http://instagram.com/hollyworton), you may have noticed that this is one of my favorite ways of reconnecting with nature, with myself, and with my intuition. Walking alone in the woods puts me in what I call a state of mobile meditation, where everything clears out of my mind and I enter into flow. The important detail here is that I go walking alone: my intuition doesn't pop up if I'm out with a group of people, or even with just one other person. Trail running is also great for this.

Have you ever been driving and suddenly realized you don't remember the last ten minutes of your trip? It's like that. I'm aware of staying on the trail and I'm conscious of where I'm going, but my mind just relaxes and lets go of all the chatter. It's also safer than zoning out while operating a vehicle—obviously, I don't recommend doing that.

## Get some exercise

I used to run a lot, and I found that my intuition would speak up to me when I was running. I find this easier when running on a treadmill in the gym rather than out in the street or on a trail, because these are situations where I need to be more alert of my surroundings. But you may find that running outdoors works best for you. I've recently got into trail running, and I find that it does wonders for clearing my head—even though I have to stay alert for others on the trails, like cyclists and dog walkers.

Pay attention the next time you exercise—whether it's running or something else. See which exercises help you get into that state of flow where your intuition is able to speak up more clearly. Find what works for you, and use it consciously as a time to let your intuition speak up.


## Do something repetitive

One of the reasons I think exercise is so powerful for allowing us to tune into our intuition is that it's repetitive. I'm not talking crunches or lifting weights or exercises that you need to count, because the act of counting can distract you from the intuitive messages that may be trying to come in. I'm referring to running, or using the elliptical trainer, or stair-stepper, or something like that.

Try doing something repetitive outside of the gym, like chopping vegetables for a meal, knitting, or pulling weeds in the garden. Repetitive physical actions can calm your conscious mind and open up space for your intuition to speak up. Again, go with simple tasks.

One of the reasons I never ventured beyond knitting scarves was because scarves were such repetitive work. I would find myself repeating the stitches like a mantra—

"knit, knit, knit backward, purl" still sticks in my mind. I once attempted a sock, but was put off by all the row counting I had to do to follow the pattern.

These are all excellent ways to quiet your mind and allow your intuition to speak up.

## Drive aimlessly

This is not something that I ever do, but I know that it's a great technique for many people. Hop in your car and just drive, with no direction. You may find that back country roads are better than urban areas for getting your mind into a quieter state that you need for your intuition to speak to you, but go with what works for you. Obviously, you'll need to be a responsible driver and pay attention to what's going on around you.

Also be aware that it will be a bit challenging to record the messages from your intuition. You may need to pull to the side of the road or park to write things down. Bring a pen and paper or your phone and record the messages from your intuition when you stop driving.

## Get creative

Being creative is one of the most common ways of letting intuition come through, especially if you can manage to be in a state of flow when you're being creative. I'm talking about drawing, painting, dancing, writing, playing music -- however it is that you let your creative juices flow.

Coloring in those adult coloring books that are so popular these days can be a good way of putting our conscious mind to rest and accessing our intuition. Drawing mandalas is another good way of doing this, and it can also be seen as a form of meditation. Google "mandala meditation" to learn more.

When I paint, I do it from a state of flow, and not from a conscious place. That means that I don't usually know what I'm painting when I start out with a blank canvas or sheet of paper. I just start: I pick up a brush, add some paint, and little by little the images appear. It's very much an automatic process, and I've found that it helps me get into a state where my intuition can send me messages.

## Get in flow

There are so many ways to get into a state of flow: you may use exercise, being creative, or something else. I'm sure you've experienced flow before. It's also known as "the zone", and is described as a mental state in which a person is completely absorbed in a particular activity. When we're in flow, it's easier for our intuition to speak up and for us to actually hear it.

My friend Cathy Ballard has created a system that she calls the Flow Process that helps you to get into a state of flow more easily. You can learn more and download a free fifteen minute introduction to the Flow Process on her website: http://www.cathyballard.com/.

Another friend of mine, C Wilson Meloncelli, has created a very different system to access the flow state called the Elite Flow Program. You can learn more and download a free course to help you hack into the flow state on his website: http://www.cwilsonmeloncelli.com/.

## Write in a journal

There are so many things you can do with your journal that can help you get into a state where your intuition pops up and speaks to you. You can write engage in free writing, where you simply record whatever comes to mind. You can write morning pages, which are three pages of longhand, stream of consciousness writing done first thing in the morning. You can handwrite on paper or type into a file on your computer. Do whatever works for you.

Journaling can help you to tune into yourself and reconnect with yourself. You can also ask yourself questions, and then journal the answers based on what pops into your mind.

My journal contains all kinds of things, including my gratitude lists. Whenever I want to break out of an icky state, or clear my mind, or get ready to be creative, or start a new project, I write a list of ten things I'm grateful for, and why. Gratitude lists can help you get into a state where your intuition comes through more easily.

## Feel into your body

This is something that I'm not very good about remembering to do, except when I'm actually getting an intuitive gut feeling about something. One of the ways intuition speaks to us is through your body, and the more we cultivate awareness of what's going on with our body, the more sensitive we become to these messages.

You can make it easier to do this by trying a body scan, where you place your attention on each part of your body, starting at one end and working your way to the other. There are many guided meditations online that walk you through this. Just do a search for "body scan meditation."

If you get an uncomfortable physical sensation when you're trying to make a decision, pay close attention to it. Do you feel a tightness in your chest or a sick feeling in your gut? Does the decision you're about to make feel light or heavy to you?

If you can remember to stop for a moment and feel into your body when making decisions, your intuition can give you physical clues as to which is the best path to follow. This is where following your heart or your gut feeling come into play. Remember, when I'm talking about your heart I'm referring to your intuition, not your emotions.

## Flip a coin

My husband and I use this all the time to make simple decisions, like what film to watch or what to have for dinner. When we're feeling stuck and we're not sure what we want, we flip a coin. One person picks a side, and the other person flips (usually him; I'm terrible at flipping a coin).

We go for the best two out of three, and when the final result comes up, we'll both usually get an instant gut feeling as to whether we're happy with the outcome or not. Obviously, we go with what our gut says, not with the outcome of the coin toss. We use the coin as a tool to activate that gut feeling, and it makes the process fun.

## Muscle testing

I discuss muscle testing extensively in my first book, *Business Beliefs*, where I discuss how to use muscle testing to access your subconscious mind and see which beliefs you hold at the subconscious level. I also have a quick video on my YouTube channel that explains how to do self muscle testing, but you may want to read more about how to actually implement that in your business.

For example, I used to offer free Pricing Calls to entrepreneurs who were struggling to set prices that feel aligned with the value of their products and services. In these calls, I used muscle testing to help business owners determine the best prices for their offerings. Usually, the prices that tested strong are the ones that their intuition already came up with, but their head decided were wrong for whatever reason. I find that receiving the clear message through muscle testing helps these entrepreneurs give themselves permission to set the best prices for them.

I always warn that it's important to not give your power away to the process of muscle testing. In the same way that I take the outcome of the coin toss and use it to see what my gut feeling is about something, we can use the information we gain from muscle testing to make conscious decisions in our business. Muscle testing is a fantastic way of tapping into our subconscious to see which beliefs it holds, and it's also a great way to access the wisdom of our higher self, which is where I believe our intuition comes from.

**Use oracle cards**

Like tossing a coin or using muscle testing, another way to access our intuition is by using oracle cards or tarot cards. You can ask a question, then choose a card as the answer. You can ask for guidance on a particular topic, and then pull a card. Most often, I find that the card I pull is totally resonant and makes absolute sense. My gut confirms that the information or concept represented by the card is right for me.

But if you pull a card and it doesn't resonate, that's another clear message from your intuition that something's not quite right. Is your head getting in the way? Is there something you're afraid of? One year, when I pulled my twelve oracle cards, one for each month of the year, I got a card that scared me. So I put it back in the deck and pulled another one. That one didn't make sense. And when that month rolled around, almost an entire year later, I knew that it was the original oracle card that was right, not the second one. But my head got in the way of my gut.

## Ask a question

Sit in a quiet place where you won't be disturbed and ask a question, either out loud or silently, in your mind. Wait patiently for the answer. If you don't get one, then answer it yourself, and imagine yourself following through with one or more of the options.

For example, if you're struggling to decide whether to sign up for a new online course, and you ask whether it's the right thing for your business at this time and don't hear an answer, imagine yourself taking the course. How does that feel? Does it feel right, or does something feel off about it? Then imagine yourself opting not to sign up to the course. How does that feel? Does it feel right, or not?

## Take a bath or shower

Bathing can put us in a state of relaxation that helps our intuitive messages to come through. Earlier in this book I mentioned "shower thoughts," those little nuggets of inner wisdom that come in when our minds are focused on what's usually the automatic process of cleansing our bodies. When our conscious minds are engaged, intuition is more likely to pop through and be heard.

## Go on a retreat

Going on a solo retreat can also give you the space you need for your intuition to speak up. Whether it's going away to meditate, do yoga, exercise, or simply going on a long distance walk, a retreat can be a good way of reconnecting with our intuition. When I walked one hundred miles from Winchester to Eastbourne along the South Downs Way, it put me in a much deeper state of mobile meditation than I normally get from a single day's walk.

While I regularly do workcation weekends, I have on occasion changed plans and used my "workcation" as a personal retreat instead. Usually that's when my gut is telling me that I need to take some time off. These have been great opportunities to let my intuition speak up.

I can get the same results from a solo camping trip. By getting out in nature and slowing down to its rhythms, it helps me to quiet my mind so my intuition can speak up.

## Be silent

For years, I wanted to go on a silent retreat, ever since a friend of mine told me of a weekend retreat she did at a silent monastery. Finally, a couple of years ago, my friend Cathy Ballard and I created our own silent retreat. We found a quiet old farmhouse on Airbnb and we spent two nights and three days there. We created our own schedule of activities, and we spent the whole time in silence.

It was incredibly powerful. So many fears and limiting beliefs were brought to light, which I detailed in a blog post titled "My Celery is Good Enough." I was able to work on those things and clear them from my mindset.

And I was also able to listen to the voice of my intuition, which came up loud and clear through art journaling and other silent activities. Freeing ourselves of the need to speak can put us in a place where we're more likely to listen to our intuition when it speaks to us.

## Be alone

Alone time is just as powerful—if not more so—than silent time with someone else. When we're alone, we don't have the distraction of other people. You can go on a solo walk, run, retreat, or something else. Or you can simply sit at home, alone in a chair or on your bed. Relax. And tune into the messages from your intuition.

## Read books

Read other books about how to develop your intuition. The book *365 Ways to Connect With Your Soul* was edited by Jodi Chapman and Dan Tech, and was written by over 200 contributors, including myself. It's got, as the name implies, 365 ways to access your intuition—one for each day of the year. There's also Sonia Choquette's *Trust Your Vibes*, Shakti Gawain's *Developing Intuition*, and Caroline Myss's *Sacred Contracts*.

## Notice pattens

When things start showing up over and over, take note. This may be your intuition speaking up by pointing your attention to something again and again. If three different people recommend the same book to you, buy it and read it.

The same goes for thoughts. If you keep thinking of a certain place that you've been, figure out what that place gave you, and see how you can meet that need in your life. If you keep thinking of a certain person, maybe there's a reason. Reach out and get in touch. Or get clear on what that relationship gives you and see how you can meet it in your life today.

## Sleep

This is probably one of the most passive methods of accessing our intuition, but taking advantage of sleep time usually involves setting the stage to get messages while we sleep. You can set the intention to get an answer to a problem or situation in your dreams, and then wait to consciously receive the answer once you wake up.

It's important to remember that you've set this intention upon waking, otherwise you might forget anything that's come through during the night. It may help to have a notebook by your bed, and make note of any and all dreams you had during the night. Sometimes, the intuitive message is just a small part of a larger dream that you can only access by writing the whole thing down.

$\sim$

## Step 3: Turn up the volume

That was a very extensive list of ways you can tune into your intuition. As I've mentioned before, your intuition will often show up at first as a tiny whisper, which can be easy to ignore because it's so subtle. In fact, you'll probably miss it the first few times it comes through. In order to make accessing your business intuition easier, you'll need to turn up the volume. As you may have imagined, there are many ways to do this, and you can try one or all of the suggestions below.

## Tune in

All of the suggestions I gave above for tuning into your intuition can also be used to strengthen it even more. You may have noticed that most of the methods involve quiet alone time. The more you can give yourself time to be alone in a quiet, relaxed space, the stronger your intuitive voice will become.

## Make time

Block off time in your calendar every day or every week where you can be alone in a quiet, relaxed space where you can allow your intuitive messages to come in. Set the intention of really paying attention to your intuition when it speaks up, and be sure to listen when it does. Before long, that whisper will grow louder, and will be easier to hear.

You can also block off time to engage in any of the other intuition-developing activities that I mentioned earlier in the chapter. Remember that if you want to turn up the volume on your intuition, you're going to need to make the time and the space to develop this tool, just like you would if you were learning a new instrument or practicing a new sport. This is essentially a mental muscle that you're developing.

## Take immediate action

One of the ways I've learned to turn up the volume on my intuition is to take immediate action on the messages when they pop up. When I don't take immediate action, I tend to forget the message, and this only serves to weaken the voice of my intuition. For example, when I described overriding the suggestion of my intuition to bring my video bag because my head, or conscious mind, told me not to get distracted, this was a missed opportunity to strengthen the voice of my intuition by listening to its advice.

## Stop asking for advice

Another way to strengthen your intuition is to stop asking for advice from other people. You might want to challenge yourself to go advice-free for one month (or longer) as you're turning up the volume on your intuition. As I said earlier, advice isn't bad—but if you can learn to turn up the volume on your intuition, that's something you'll always have within yourself.

## Record the messages

Of course, it's not always possible to take immediate action when our intuition speaks up. But it is often possible to make note of the messages. I have a page in my business notebook where I write down all of my topics for future books, and I have a virtual notebook in Evernote where I make note of other things. You can also put the suggestion action into your to do system. This makes it easier to take action on the wisdom our intuition at a later time, when it's easier to to so.

∾

So you've made space for your intuition, you've tuned into its signal, and you've turned up the volume on its voice. Now let's have a little talk about actually trusting the messages it gives you. Trusting your intuition is another way of strengthening its voice, but this deserves a separate chapter of its own.

# 8

# TRUSTING YOUR BUSINESS INTUITION

*"I believe in intuitions and inspirations...I sometimes feel that I am right. I do not know that I am."*

— ALBERT EINSTEIN

When we trust our business intuition, we run our business very differently: we instinctively know what to do, we receive immediate answers to our questions, and we know exactly what's right for us. It's not enough to listen to the little whisper of our intuition; we've got to trust it enough to take action on what it's telling us to do.

But we've got to *learn* to trust it, and that can be challenging when we've spent so much of our lives trusting our head. I've always been a sucker for logic: when making decisions, my head would always search for the logical answer. It should come as no surprise that my favorite Star Trek character is Spock. And that's why my head, or my conscious mind, so often gets in the way of receiving and acting on the messages my subconscious has for me.

Your intuition comes from within yourself, so trusting your intuition is all about trusting yourself. Learning to trust yourself can be challenging, especially if we've made decisions in the past that have impacted our business or life in a difficult way. It takes some work to learn to trust yourself and your intuition, but it can be done—I'm proof of this.

## How to trust yourself

It may take time to cultivate a strong sense of self trust, which will then reinforce your trust in your intuition. Be patient with yourself throughout this process. As with everything else I've discussed in this book, there are many ways to learn to trust yourself, and you can try one or all of the suggestions below.

## Make the decision

Make a conscious decision to trust yourself. Set the intention. This is the simplest and easiest place to start. How does this work? Simply say to yourself, or write in your journal, something along the lines of: "I choose to trust myself and to increase my self trust."

I know that sounds too easy, too good to be true. But it's a great starting point, because it clarifies your intention. It gives you something to focus on. Honoring the power of your choice to trust yourself is important. Are you ready, willing, and able to trust yourself? Then set the intention now.

If you use PSYCH-K® or other processes to reprogram your subconscious mind, you might want to create a belief statement such as "I choose to trust myself and to increase my self trust" or "I easily trust myself every day in every way" and then program that into your subconscious.

## Declutter again

Our decluttering is never done, because if we dig deeper, we can always find more things to let go of. Plus, we're constantly accumulating new things that we may need to release in the future. When we let go of negative messages we may have received earlier in our lives, including beliefs we may have formed during our childhood, this can help us develop a greater sense of self trust. This includes releasing any stress, trauma, or fears we may have. Again, I use PSYCH-K® to do this because that's what works best for me, but it's important for you find the process or technique that works best for *you.*

If you want to declutter some more, but are feeling stuck on how to declutter the emotional and mental stuff, do another physical declutter of your office and home. That can serve to free up things in our minds as well. Once we've cleared up the stuff that no longer serves us, both physically, mentally, and emotionally, it makes it easier for us to trust ourselves.

## Take responsibility

By taking responsibility for your actions, you develop a greater sense of self trust. Sometimes we make "good" decisions that bring a desired outcome, and sometimes we make "bad" decisions that bring about an unexpected and undesired outcome, creating new challenges in our lives. But regardless of the outcome, we get that result based on decisions that we've made.

When we blame others for an undesired outcome, we're

giving our power away to them. We're temporarily relieving the pain of the experience, but at the same time we're creating a much bigger problem by not taking responsibility for the decisions we make. And when we don't take responsibility for our decisions, we damage our self trust a little bit more.

Moving from blaming others to taking responsibility requires a major mindset shift, and it can take time to reprogram our minds to do this. (It is, however, much quicker when we make the mindset changes at the subconscious level rather than at the conscious level.) However, when we eventually take full responsibility for our actions and decisions, it makes it much, much easier for us to trust ourselves.

If you use PSYCH-K® or other techniques to reprogram your subconscious mind, you might want to create a belief statement such as "I forgive myself and others for all the wrongs done to me and I take responsibility for my own life" and then program that into your subconscious. That particular statement comes from the PSYCH-K® Basic Workshop manual, and it's such a powerful belief to hold.

## Speak your truth

"Speak your truth" is a coachy, feel-good, new-agey kind of term. But all it really means is telling the truth as you see it. When someone asks for your opinion, or what you want to do, or what you believe/think/feel/want/need, you speak the truth. *Your* truth. When we speak our truth, it teaches ourselves that we can be trusted to take care of ourselves by voicing our beliefs, thoughts, feelings wants, and needs.

It requires you to acknowledge what you believe/think/feel/want/need and to be honest about that when sharing it with others. It involves taking responsibility for your beliefs, thoughts, and feelings and recognizing that they may or may not be well received. It means that despite the fact that your truth may not be well received, you share it anyway.

Let me clarify something here: I'm not talking about being painfully honest when it hurts someone else, or telling someone something about them that could be considered insensitive. I'm talking about *you* speaking *your* truth about *your* stuff. That's an important detail.

In your personal life, this is about being honest when a friend suggests you go to an Italian restaurant for dinner, and you know that pasta makes you feel awful. It's about speaking up and suggesting something else, because wheat just doesn't feel good when you eat it. Not speaking your truth would be going along with the idea and eating the pasta anyway.

In your business life, this is about speaking up when your graphic designer delivers something that isn't quite right. Perhaps they completely ignored part of your design brief, or maybe you weren't quite specific enough on certain details. Either way, it's important that you take responsibility, and speak your truth by giving them clear feedback on what you'd rather have instead. Not speaking your truth would be accepting the first draft of the design and using it anyway.

When we speak our truth, it makes it easier for us to trust ourselves because we're taking responsibility for our beliefs, thoughts, feelings, wants, and needs.

## Uphold your boundaries

Along the same lines of speaking our truth is upholding our boundaries. We set our boundaries to maintain balance in our lives and to protect ourselves from the behavior or demands of others. When we uphold our boundaries, it teaches us that we can be trusted to set boundaries and maintain them. It also teaches us self respect, because we can be relied upon to respect those boundaries.

In your business life, this involves creating a coaching contract or service agreement that details your business boundaries and then upholding those boundaries when a client oversteps them. For example, if a client arrives late for an appointment, they may lose that time rather than you extending the session at the end. If a client is later than a certain amount of time, such as fifteen minutes, you might cancel the session entirely and consider it to be a missed session.

The importance of setting these boundaries is that you then uphold them if the situation arises, if it's appropriate to do so. Not upholding your boundaries would mean giving in and rescheduling the session for the missed appointment because you don't want the client to get upset or angry with you. (Having said that, I don't believe that rules should never be broken, and there are certainly instances when a client is late for a session or misses a session entirely, and it's perfectly understandable...in the event of a personal or family emergency, for example.)

When we uphold our boundaries, it makes it easier for us to trust ourselves, because we know we're reliable.

### Practice self care

Self care is simply taking care of ourselves and respecting our needs, whatever that means to each of us. It can be seen as a method of self protection to ensure that we do not place too many demands on ourselves. When we practice self care, and take care of ourselves, we make sure that we have everything that we need to experience balance and wellbeing in our lives.

This may look like getting enough sleep, making sure you have plenty of time to eat unhurried meals, and making time in your schedule for exercise. It may involve reading a good book in the bath to relax at the end of the day, or it may include observing strict working hours with full weekends off. Self care will be different for everyone.

In your business life, this may involve not staying away from the computer on weekends, or closing your office door after business hours, or not answering emails on your phone. We could have a whole conversation about business boundaries, and I may eventually write a book about this, but essentially they're all about taking care of yourself by not letting your business overcome your entire existence.

When you don't practice self care by upholding your these personal boundaries, you can get stressed out and overwhelmed. It also damages your self trust, because deep down you know you can't be trusted to take care of yourself. And when you can't be trusted to take care of yourself, who can be trusted to take care of you? No one.

When we practice self care, it makes it easier for us to trust ourselves, because deep down, we know that we make a habit of taking care of our needs.

## Keep promises to yourself

It's important to keep our promises to ourselves, whenever possible. By keeping our promises we're teaching ourselves that we can be trusted, and that we take ourselves seriously. We can be depended on to look out for our needs and wants, and not just the needs and wants of others.

The promises you make to yourself might involve any of the things we've already discussed, like deciding to declutter our homes or our beliefs, taking responsibility for our decisions and actions, speaking our truth, upholding our boundaries, or practicing self care. They might involve setting clear business goals and working to achieve them. The important thing here is that when we make a promise to ourselves, we keep it. Keeping our promises to ourselves makes it easier for us to trust ourselves.

## Finish what you start

Finishing what you start goes along with keeping the promises you make to yourself. If you've decided that you want to do something that's important to you, then make sure you complete it. When we finish what we started, it makes it easier for us to trust ourselves because we know deep down that we'll make it happen.

However, if you're halfway through a project and circumstances change, your intuition may send you a message that it's time to let go. Maybe you've acquired new information, or perhaps you've realized that this project isn't the right thing for you, after all. If that's the case, be open and willing to let go and move onto something else.

There are no hard rules with intuition, and sometimes things change and we need to be able to make changes to the original plan and move on. And that's okay. This may sound tricky, but once you get used to listening to your intuition and trusting it, you'll know when to let go and move onto something else, and when your mind is simply coming up with excuses for you to not get the work done.

## Value yourself

When we value ourselves, it makes it easier for us to trust ourselves. I'm fully aware that this isn't easy for a lot of us.

I've had to do a lot of mindset work around valuing who I am and what I know, and I've done so much work with my clients to help them do the same. Self worth is a big issue for many entrepreneurs, and it may be something that you need to do additional work on.

But when you value yourself, you value all aspects of your being, including your intuition. And the more you value your intuition, the louder it will speak to you. That's just reinforcing what you want.

Now, even though you've worked on trusting your business intuition and trusting yourself, you might still find it challenging. In the next chapter, we're going to explore all the little things that can block the voice of your intuition or gut feeling.

# 9

# THINGS THAT CLOUD INTUITION

"Each of us must confront our own fears, must come face to face with them. How we handle our fears will determine where we go with the rest of our lives. To experience adventure or to be limited by the fear of it."

— JUDY BLUME

There are all kinds of nasty things that can cloud our intuition: fears, blocks, and limiting beliefs. These are the mind gremlins I spoke of earlier. This is your inner critic and also the stuff that keeps you stuck in your comfort zone.

These are also things that can be cleared up quickly and easily, if you know how. I discuss all kinds of business blocks in my book titled, aptly, *Business Blocks*. You might find that useful. But let's focus here on intuition fears, blocks, and limiting beliefs.

## Fears

What fears do you have around following your intuition? Do you think it's dangerous to trust your gut? Do you think it's dangerous to trust yourself? Are you afraid you'll make the wrong decisions, and then everyone will say "I told you so" because it was obvious your decision was illogical? What's the worst that could happen if you threw logic aside and trusted your gut?

## Blocks

What's keeping you stuck in developing your intuition? What's the benefit to remain deaf to the messages of your gut? How is ignoring your intuition keeping you safe?

## Limiting beliefs

What limiting beliefs do you have around trusting your intuition? Do you believe that logic is most important? Do you believe that only woo-woo people trust their gut over logic? Do you believe that it's dangerous to give your gut priority over your head?

## Mindset work

Clearing these fears, blocks, and limiting beliefs is the basis of the mindset work that I used to do. It's work that you can do on your own, or with another professional. As I said before, I find it most useful to do both: work with myself and with someone else.

Here's how to get started:

1. Identify the core intuition blocks that you need

to shift in your mindset, using the methods and questions described in this chapter. Get my first books, *Business Beliefs* and *Business Blocks*, and work through those books to get even more clarity.

2. Find the best technique for you to change your mindset at the subconscious level.
3. Find the best practitioner or facilitator to help you with this mindset transformation, and/or do the work yourself.
4. Do the inner work to transform your mindset.
5. Take action to reinforce your new mindset.
6. Repeat.

**1. Identify the blocks you need to shift**

Identify the fears and blocks that have around using your intuition, using the methods described in this chapter. Spend time journaling to get clear on what you *do* want to experience in terms of using your intuition in your business, and which fears, blocks, and limiting beliefs you need to release in order to make that happen.

**2 and 3. Find the best process and practitioner**

This may involve trial and error. If something doesn't feel quite right, then don't go back again. You don't owe them anything. Listen to your gut feeling on this, and if you don't see changes reasonably soon, you might want to reevaluate whether you've found the best method (or practitioner) for you.

There are many processes and techniques out there, and there are many facilitators and practitioners of each one. Sometimes it can be tricky to find what's right for you.

It can take trial and error. That's why I haven't included a specific process in this book: what works for me may or may not work for you.

Some of the processes and techniques you might like to try include:

- Heart-centered Energy Work®
- PSYCH-K®
- ThetaHealing®
- Emotional Freedom Techniques® (EFT or tapping)
- NLP (Neuro-Linguistic Programming)
- TAT (Tapas Acupressure Technique)
- Ask & Receive
- hypnotherapy
- ...and more

I've also experienced sound therapy sessions and light language sessions. In 2019, I graduated from a Shamanic Plant Spirit Healing Apprenticeship, which does what it says in the name: it taught me how to work with plant spirits for healing (which, of course, can also help to free ourselves from our blocks).

Different types of healing can also help us connect with our intuition: I find that a relaxing session of reiki or other energy healing can leave me rested, refreshed, and ready to receive intuitive messages.

Change can be *fast* when you're working at the subconscious and energetic levels, so there's no need to attend weekly sessions for months before seeing results. Stay alert, and pay attention to how your intuition is different since you started doing the mindset work. How has it improved? Sometimes significant changes occur, but people don't notice because things are going well, and they're no longer experiencing whatever it was that they wanted to let go of. That's why it's so useful to write things down in a journal.

## 4. Do the training yourself

I always recommend that people train in a process or technique themselves so they can do the work on their own. There is great power in being able to release your blocks whenever you want, wherever you want, however you want. I have spent the past several years working on my blocks regularly (at least once a week!), and I also see other professionals from time to time. In my experience, this is the perfect combination to approach releasing our business blocks.

If you've found a process that you particularly like, train in it and learn how to do it for yourself. This will require an initial investment, but it will save you time and money in the long run. You'll be able to make significant changes in your belief system, and you'll be reaping the results in your business. This process is what I mean when I say "do the inner work."

## 5. Take inspired action

When I work with clients, I always help them create a short action plan at the end of each session. This is important: no matter how much work we do to release our blocks and transform our mindset, we also have to take practical action. We can release as many blocks as we want, but if we don't *do the work* to develop our intuition, we won't automatically create change.

So remember to stay on top of your intuition-building practices. Make the time and space to listen to the voice of your intuition. Do the work to turn up the volume of the messages.

I always say this is like climbing a spiral staircase: the left step is the mindset work; the right step is the practical action. Left, right, left, right, and up we go as we build our business.

In a later chapter, I talk a little bit about how you can work with others on your mindset if you feel drawn to do so. If not, I encourage you to read through the chapter, so you can at least have some point of comparison to other professionals that you may choose to work with. It helps to have an idea of how different people work so you can find what's best for you.

Remember: *you* know what's best for you! There's a reason I keep saying this: we can have the tendency to give our power away to others, but deep down, you're the one who knows what's best. Go with your gut feeling!

# 10

# BUSINESS INTUITION BELIEF STATEMENTS

*"If you want to have an intuitive life, you have to have the courage to be open to who you are."*

— SONIA CHOQUETTE

The way that I used to work with entrepreneurs was with a process called PSYCH-K®, which helps to reprogram beliefs at the subconscious level, allowing us to release fears, blocks, and limiting beliefs and reinforce positive, enhancing beliefs. When we're programming enhancing (positive) beliefs, we often use belief statements to do so. Belief statements are short statements, kind of like affirmations: they're stated in the present tense, and are focused on what we do want, not what we don't want.

If you've read my first book, *Business Beliefs*, then you've learned how to use muscle testing to access your subconscious mind and see which beliefs you hold at the subconscious level. If you know how to use muscle testing, then you may find it useful to see what beliefs you currently hold around business intuition. I'm including a list of sample beliefs below. You can change the language on any of the belief statements so that they sound like something you'd write or say. It's important that the language feel like it's yours.

If you find that you don't currently believe any or all of these statements at the subconscious level, you might want to do some work to transform your beliefs. There are many ways you could do this: by working with a practitioner or therapist or by doing the work with yourself. I recommend a combination of the two: I regularly use PSYCH-K® with myself to transform my business mindset, but I also work with another PSYCH-K® facilitator to help me uncover my blocks and get to the core of what's going on for me.

It's important that you find the technique that works best for you. That could be PSYCH-K®, or it could be NLP, EFT, TAT, hypnotherapy, or something else. You might need to try a few different techniques before you find what works for you. I include PSYCH-K® as an example in a lot of my stories because that's what works for me.

## Belief Statements

1. Listening to my intuition is easy and effortless.
2. I am confident in the wisdom of my intuition.
3. I easily listen to and follow the wisdom of my intuition.
4. I have full trust and belief in my intuition.
5. I easily follow my gut feelings.
6. Listening to my intuition makes me feel confident in my decisions.
7. I am ready, willing, and able to follow my intuition.

8. I have the courage to listen to and take action on the messages from my intuition.
9. I can rely on my intuition and I regularly do.
10. I am open to hearing the messages that my intuition brings me.
11. I trust each and every decision I make with my intuition.
12. It's safe and appropriate for me to listen to my intuition.
13. I have full faith in my intuition.
14. I always pay attention to my intuition and take action on it.
15. I easily turn up the volume on the whisper of my intuition.
16. It's easy for me to hear the voice of my intuition.
17. I value my intuition more than I value logic.
18. My mind is filled with intuitive wisdom.
19. My creativity is strengthened by intuitive ideas.
20. Intuitive wisdom comes to me easily and effortlessly.
21. It's easy for me to develop my intuition and I do.
22. Listening to my intuition gives me a great sense of security.
23. I easily learn from my intuitive messages.
24. I feel safe and confident when I make decisions based on my intuition.
25. My intuition tells me which business tasks are the highest priority.
26. I easily know if an opportunity is good for me and quickly take action.
27. I have crystal clarity of mind and easily hear the voice of my intuition.
28. The more I listen to my intuition, the louder it speaks to me.

29. I feel deeply satisfied when I make decisions based on my intuition.
30. I easily make snap decisions based on the wisdom of my intuition.
31. I easily say no to things that my gut tells me aren't right for me.
32. My intuition allows me to focus with laser clarity on the right things.
33. My intuition guides me to easily take action on the highest priority actions.
34. The more I listen to my intuition, the easier my life is.
35. When I listen to my intuition, my business becomes easy and effortless.

# 11

# TAKE INSPIRED ACTION

*"It is always with excitement that I wake up in the morning wondering what my intuition will toss up to me, like gifts from the sea. I work with it and rely on it. It's my partner."*

— JONAS SALK

I hope this book has inspired you to take action to hone your business intuition. Of course, when you work to improve your inner wisdom, it doesn't just affect your business intuition, but rather helps you receive messages that will assist you in all aspects of your life. It's like having your own personal advisor that always knows what's best for you.

And like I said earlier, your intuition makes it easy for you to see the next best action to take on the path toward your goals. Sometimes, it can be hard to see every single step that we need to take, but when we're confident that our next best step is the right one, it makes it easier to follow the path.

I've already given you loads of tips on how to take

action to hone your business intuition, but let's break it down into super simple steps:

**1. Develop your intuition.**

You may remember that this is a three step process: make space, tune in, and turn up the volume. I give you five different ways to make space for your intuitive messages to come through, nineteen ways to tune into your inner wisdom, and three ways to turn up the volume on the voice of your intuition. Try one method from each category, or try all of them and see what works best for you.

**2. Trust your intuition.**

I share several ways to help you trust your intuition. When you trust your inner wisdom, it allows you to take action on the messages you receive and it helps to strengthen the signals that your intuition sends you.

**3. Take inspired action.**

Business involves more than just sitting back and receiving messages from your inner wisdom. You need to take action to make things happen, and the more action you take that's based on the messages your intuition has sent you, the easier it will be to receive more of those messages in the future. Taking action based on intuitive guidance is one of the best ways to really reinforce your intuitive wisdom.

**4. Remove any blocks.**

Do you have any fears, blocks, or limiting beliefs around your intuition? If you become aware of these, it's important to do the mindset work to transform your beliefs and release your blocks. That will help you to receive guidance more clearly.

**5. Repeat.**

Developing your intuition is a process, and as you take steps to improve your inner guidance, you may find that you reach a ceiling, plateau, or upper limit on how much information you receive, or how clear are the messages. By following these steps once again from the top, you can easily improve your business intuition even more.

∾

SEE HOW EASY THAT IS? Get started with step one, and work your way through the steps. I guarantee your intuition will improve.

# 12

# HOW TO USE INTUITION IN YOUR BUSINESS

*"I told you so."*

— YOUR INTUITION

I'm being silly with this chapter's quote, but let's be honest: how many times have you heard your intuition speak, you ignored its advice, and then regretted it later? I hope that this book has inspired you to stop ignoring the advice that your higher self is so graciously giving you. Taking action on your intuitive messages can be a powerful way to easily and effortlessly take action toward your goals.

There are so many ways to use your intuition in your business, but they all boil down to easily and effortlessly making the right decisions: the kind of decisions that are 100% aligned with your best interest and highest good. Listening to your intuition and following its advice just makes everything easier, and not listening to it can lead to regret. Here are some examples of how you can use it in business:

### 1. Clarify your dreams.

Sometimes, it's hard to get clear on the big vision we have for our business (I actually have a free resource that you can use to get clear on your Big Business Vision), and tuning into your intuition can help with this. Give yourself the time and space to receive those messages that will help you to get more details on exactly what you want in your business and life.

### 2. Hone in on your Big Why.

It's important to know *why* you're running your business, because that Big Why can help you to stay on track even when things get tough. It keeps you motivated, and it makes moving toward your goals much easier. Your intuition can help you clarify exactly *why* you're doing what you're doing with your business.

### 3. Hire the best people.

Taking on staff, whether freelance or full time, can be difficult. It can be really hard to hire the right people, and I know I've made bad hiring decisions in the past. Your intuition can help you get the right people on board with your business.

### 4. Quickly solve problems.

When you hit a challenge in your business, or when things don't go quite as you planned, your intuition can give you the clarity you need to quickly solve the problem and move on.

## 5. Easily plan your strategy.

In the same way that your intuition helps you to clarify your dreams, it can also help you to plan your strategy by giving you valuable information regarding the best way to grow your business and achieve your goals.

## 6. Let go of things.

When things aren't quite right for us, our intuition can give us the message that it's time to let go. While this can be difficult for many people, it's much easier to release something that's not right for us when we have that intuitive confirmation that it's time to move on.

## 7. Be creative.

Your intuition can give you inspiration on how to be creative in your business. It can help you to create powerful content, and it can help you find new ways to express yourself.

## 8. Forge your own path.

Sometimes we need to be brave and do something completely different and new: something that we've never done before, or something that's never been done in our industry. That can be scary, but when we have clear messages from our intuition that this is the right path for us, that can make it easier to do something wildly new and different.

~

I HOPE that this book has helped give you a clear idea of why listening to your business intuition is so important, and how to develop the skill so you can easily receive valuable messages that will help you grow your business more quickly and easily. If you feel like you might need a bit more help actually making this happen, I'll let you know how you can get that assistance in the next chapter.

# 13

# NEED MORE HELP?

### Feeling stuck?

I f you've read this book, and are still feeling like you need more help engaging the power of your inner wisdom, read on. Or perhaps you've taken the five inspired action steps, and you uncovered some fears, blocks, or limiting beliefs that have gotten in the way of you honing your business intuition. If that's the case, I can help.

### Is this you?

Are you a coach, a healer, or a holistic therapist? Maybe you've got another type of business, and you're on a mission to change the world through the work that you do. You may be just starting out in business, or you may be in the process of growing your existing business.

But you've hit a rough spot. You've done all the business and marketing training, but somehow things just aren't flowing for you. You're feeling stuck. Frustrated.

All you want is more clients so you can help more

people (and, let's face it, make a decent living from your business). You're starting to realize that being successful in business isn't just about knowing how to market and run a business. It's also about your mindset: making sure that your beliefs and your inner dialogue are aligned with your vision and goals.

But it's not always that easy, is it?

**Maybe you're struggling with:**

- Lack of confidence, which leads to you procrastinating on getting your Most Important Tasks completed.
- Fear that people won't get what you do. They won't want it, or else they won't be willing to pay you for it.
- Issues around visibility and fear of standing out in the online crowd.
- Fear of overwhelm if you actually do attract all the clients you want and build a thriving business.
- Getting started with social media marketing, speaking, videos, and webinars...the thought of any of this makes you cringe.
- Believing you have something really valuable to offer. I mean, you know you do, but...do you really?

**Have you ever experienced any of this?**

If so, you're not alone. I really struggled with this stuff when I started my second business, and until I found a solution to all of this, my business suffered.

Fortunately, I found an easy solution to all of this. One that's fast, effective, and painless. It transformed my business and it transformed my life.

**Imagine how it would feel if:**

- You only attracted great clients: people who know what they want and they value what you do.
- You felt nourished and fulfilled by your business, confident that you were making a difference in the world, client by client.
- You had a tribe of raving fans who were eager to sign up for your new product or service launches.
- You had a clear vision for your business that was totally aligned with your purpose: 100% you.
- Your business felt like it was in flow, with a regular stream of clients ready to invest in what you have to offer.

**Sound good?**

This is what I want for you. I want to help purpose-driven women entrepreneurs create the business of their dreams that allows them to live the lifestyle they want.

As I mentioned earlier in the book, I've stepped back from doing one-to-one sessions so I can focus on my writing. However, I do offer occasional sessions, as well as done-for-you mindset and energy work, in my Patreon community.

Head over to www.patreon.com/hollyworton and check

it out. Please get in touch if you have any questions: holly@hollyworton.com.

## One-to-one work

If you're ready to get started with one-to-one sessions right now, I have some recommendations for you. These are four women that I trust completely and often go to for sessions myself. They all work online via Skype/Zoom.

I recommend these five facilitators:

1. Cara Wilde: http://carawilde.com
2. Cazzie Dare: https://yearning4learning.co.uk/
3. Claire Baker: http://happyhealthyempowered.com/
4. Jo Trewartha: http://freeyourmindsolutions.com/
5. Sharon Lock: http://sharonlock.com

# 14

# TESTIMONIALS

I'm including testimonials from my clients so you can get an idea of the results you can achieve from doing work to transform your mindset at the subconscious level. Remember, find the best method to use for you, and find the best person for you to work with on this. There's no one solution for everyone.

I was so hopeful for results when I signed on with Holly, as I opened a business about 6 months prior. My financial and physical stress were through the roof, until Holly guided me to changing the appropriate belief statements.  I have **no more chest pain, no more heavyweight stress** on my shoulders, and **my most recent month's collections at the office was $80,000!  I am a magnet for money and success!** Thank you Holly! xo

— ELIZABETH D. WALKER DMD, MSD

I have undertaken more traditional coaching before and found it useful but I wanted to really tap into a deeper way of working – particularly accessing the subconscious level. **I found the HEW process really powerful** during each session and focussing on how I felt during the session (and afterwards) helped tap me into other things. My instinct was to work with Holly because I resonate with a lot of the points she makes in her videos and podcast and she is a really warm person. It was also important to me that I felt like Holly was working through a lot of the same issues that were coming up for me. This authenticity was really important to me. I would definitely do more work with Holly in the future and would recommend working with her to others.

— LOUISA WHITNEY

"When I first found Holly, I was struggling to get my business to a place of success. I had the foundation in place, and had done all the "right" things, but somehow, it still wasn't working ... for me. I felt like I had a mindset limitation holding me back. After my initial meeting with Holly, even before our first working session, I received $16K in unexpected personal income – debts repaid, a royalty check, a bank refund ... after only two working sessions, I booked $43K in sales for my business, and I quit my job. That was a dream I had held for over two years, and had been working for. It wasn't magic, I put the work in, had a funnel, ads and sales conversations all set, but the results from working with Holly were literally overnight, and amazing. So much so, that had you told me that this would be happening ... to me ... I would never have believed you... in a million years. Working with Holly is seriously one of the best investments in my business and my life, that I have ever made. Thanks Holly."

— Julie Languille

"Working with you has made a huge difference. In fact, I think it's made all the difference. Even if things don't feel comfortable I still persevere."

— Natasha Mann

"I've had some really beneficial results from the session. The changing of beliefs about myself is really working. For the first time since I started working for myself I have confidence in the value of my services and the prices I'm quoting. It's an amazing process."

— Gill Hunt

"Holly's assumption of unlimited potential and possibilities in her clients, gives her a laser focused ability to spot false limitations. Holly combines her skills with compassion and sensitivity which allows you to share yourself at a deep level. Her passion for Psych - K and her commitment to walk her talk makes her a leader in field. I recommend working with her in a heart beat."

— Cara Wilde

"Since working with Holly and fully owning what I'm really about my business has been going through a big change. The transformation and higher consciousness work to help entrepreneurs find their natural Flow and abundance is now taking centre stage.

It's not only easier to share what I do now because I'm just being myself, but I created a successful online programme called The Flow Project, I've been interviewed for podcasts and invited to speak at events on the topic, and opportunities to collaborate on projects incorporating spirituality in business are opening up all the time! It feels like I turned a major corner and my business has become really exciting!"

— CATHY BALLARD

"Holly, PSYCH-K and more importantly your kind, generous way of practicing it have been fundamental in my decluttering once and for all. OMG the peace I feel is amazing. What else can I say but THANK YOU.

You have really helped me to see and work on some fundamental issues that have kept me from moving forward with my business and my life. YOU are the bomb."

— BIBI F.

"Despite over the years of my own journey of personal growth and working on myself there was one major thing that just wasn't shifting, and it was a constant negative effect on my life that I could never quite break free of despite having tried lots of things. The weird thing is that the issues that Holly worked with me on just sort of dissolved. These were big issues of a traumatic nature that it felt like my emotional and physical body just didn't want to let go of – but after working with Holly these things just melted away. What's amazing is how quickly I saw this profound change."

— CATHERINE WATKIN

"I feel more confident that I will be able to develop and achieve my dream business and attract my ideal clients. I also am experiencing more clarity about how to use social media and know that I will overcome any blocks or obstacles. Since the session I do not feel that sense of fear and paralysis when I start to approach the social media format or platforms. I feel and know the changes on a physical, emotional, energetic and spiritual level. This was the best thing I could have done for myself and my business."

— JACQUELINE CONROY

Holly's process is absolutely phenomenal. I can hardly believe **how quickly things start to change** after we have a session – **I've seen results as soon as hours after working with her**! Somehow after we clear what needs to be cleared and call in what I desire I see opportunities that I missed before, move forward on ideas that I've been sitting on, and say yes to exactly the right things. It's like during a session with Holly **I realign my energy to match what I want to experience** – and so when we're done what I want can't help but appear in my world. **Absolutely magical**, do your future self a big favor and book in with Holly now!

— JOANNA HENNON

# BUSINESS BELIEFS

UPGRADE YOUR MINDSET TO OVERCOME SELF-
SABOTAGE, ACHIEVE YOUR GOALS, AND TRANSFORM
YOUR BUSINESS (AND LIFE)

The following is an excerpt from my book *Business Beliefs: Upgrade Your Mindset to Overcome Self-Sabotage, Achieve Your Goals, and Transform Your Business (and Life)*. It's available now in ebook, paperback, audiobook, and workbook formats.

∽

*"Watch your thoughts, for they become
    words,
Watch your words, for they become
    actions,
Watch your actions, for they become
    habits,
Watch your habits, for they become your
    character,
Watch your character, for it becomes
    your destiny."*

THIS QUOTE HAS BEEN MISATTRIBUTED to several people over the years, including Mahatma Gandhi, Ralph Waldo Emerson, Lao Tzu, Gautama Buddha, Bishop Beckwaith, and the father of Margaret Thatcher. The fact that it has been misattributed to so many different people shows just how powerful these words are, and what an impact they've made on a variety of very different cultures. In reality, it doesn't matter who first uttered these words (though if you're curious, according to Quote Investigator (http:// quoteinvestigator.com/tag/frank-outlaw/), the earliest evidence of this quote dates from 1977, when it was published in a Texas newspaper that attributed the words to Frank Outlaw, owner of the Bi-Lo supermarket chain).

Never heard of Frank Outlaw? That doesn't matter (although it probably does explain why people have tried to add weight to this quote by misattributing it to more famous people). What matters is that these words are valid: our thoughts and our beliefs create our reality.

Beliefs are the things that we hold to be true, whether or not they are. Beliefs are subjective. They represent an acceptance that someone or something—an idea or a concept—exists or is right, even without proof (for if we had evidence, then this acceptance would be knowledge, rather than belief). They may also indicate having trust, faith, or confidence in someone or something.

They are the foundation of our personality; they are the elements that we use to define ourselves as individuals. Different people hold different beliefs, and our unique beliefs are part of what makes us who we are. Our ability to step into our greatness and create the business and lifestyle of our dreams depends on our beliefs, which directly influence our behavior.

Beliefs come from every area and every stage of our lives: we form them based on our interactions with authority figures such as our parents, our teachers, our superiors at work. They come from our peers—friends, co-workers, family. We are continually forming beliefs based on our actions and our interactions with others. Unfortunately, however, many of our beliefs are not conscious, which is something that we'll examine in the next chapter.

If your mindset is fraught with limiting beliefs, you will struggle to build your business and create the lifestyle you want. On the other hand, if your mindset is supported by beliefs that lift you up, building your dream business will be much, much more manageable. That's why we must keep our beliefs positive and focused on what we *do* want, and not what we *don't* want. Unfortunately, most of us tend to focus on the former.

## Watch your thoughts, for they become words

We often express our limiting beliefs in our language. When our current mindset isn't serving us, and a friend asks us how our business is coming along, it can be easy to fall into a victim mentality and say things like:

- "I'm never going to make it. It's just too hard."
- "It's so hard to get clients. I don't know how anyone does it."
- "Building a business is easy for other people. I'm having such a hard time of it myself."

Have you ever heard words like these come out of your mouth? Or maybe you didn't say them. Perhaps they were just thoughts running through your head when you were silently complaining to yourself.

Or maybe you paid too much attention to your mind gremlins, who whispered things like:

- "You're not good enough. You'll never make a living with your business."
- "You're not smart enough to learn all the things you need to learn to market your business."
- "Be careful. If you get too big, people will find out you're a fraud."

Perhaps you found yourself at a business networking meeting, where someone asked you how business was going, and you replied that things were great—yet in the back of your mind, you were thinking just how hopeless you felt. I can't begin to count the times in the early days of my business where people would ask me how things were going, and I would smile and reply enthusiastically. I didn't want to jinx myself by telling the truth, so I pretended everything was fabulous.

Spoiler alert: it wasn't.

These words of self-doubt, whether spoken or unspoken, make up our mindset. Remember: your mindset can support and enhance you and your business, or it can sabotage and undermine you and your business.

## Watch your words, for they become actions

Our beliefs are directly related to our actions. If we have confidence in ourselves and if we have a mindset full of firm beliefs about our ability to create a successful business, then we're more likely to take the necessary actions to make that successful business become a reality. On the other hand, if our minds are fraught with limiting beliefs, we're more likely to procrastinate, hiding from the actions that will put us out there, make us visible, and get the clients we need to create our dream business.

A positive mindset will support you in stepping into

your greatness. A limiting mindset will keep you stuck in your smallness. Either way, your beliefs influence your actions.

I've seen it so many times with clients: one struggled to create videos for her YouTube channel, which she knew was essential to the growth of her business. She insisted that she wasn't tech-savvy. She spent hours crafting careful scripts, which she would then run through a teleprompter to read as she recorded her videos. This process took hours, and it meant that she put off doing videos as much as possible. After just one session where we focused on changing beliefs around her video creation, she was able to create inspiring, focused videos on YouTube by speaking spontaneously to the camera.

I had another client who also struggled with technology. The more she complained that she didn't know how to do tech things for her online business, the more she remained stuck. We worked on shifting her beliefs around technology, and she was able to work with her web designer to build a new website for her business quickly.

In my own experience, one thing that I've heard myself say more than once is that "I'm not good at play." I often take myself and my business too seriously, forgetting to allow space for fun, play, and joy. And of course, the more I repeat "I'm not good at play," the more truthful that statement becomes. It wasn't until I realized that play could take many forms—some of which I was already practicing—that I understood that I was a playful person and that I could add more play (and therefore more fun!) to my business.

## Watch your actions, for they become habits

And, of course, the more you continue to take the same actions, the more they become ingrained. Eventually, they're transformed into habits. You continue to take (or avoid) the same actions, and this only serves to reinforce your neural pathways, keeping you stuck in the same place.

I used to have the bad habit of procrastinating on my emails. I'm talking about messages that I had to respond to personally—emails that I couldn't delegate to an assistant or someone else. I would let them pile up for days in my inbox, and just seeing them would stress me out (though to be fair, having more than twenty emails in my inbox at a time makes me anxious!). I finally started blocking out time in my calendar regularly, where I would force myself to only work on my inbox, and that helped me to get back on track.

Even worse was my track record for returning phone calls. I've since significantly improved in this respect, but for many years I would procrastinate on making phone calls. I'd have them on my list of things to do, but often it would take me *more than a month* to make the calls. I hated phone calls that much. Often, so much time had passed that I would just cross the call off my list because it was no longer relevant.

I used to be extremely organized and tidy. For the most part, I still am, mostly because I get anxious when things are disheveled or out of place. But sometimes, I get into the habit of accumulating a pile of paperwork on my desk—and then not doing anything about it for weeks at a time. Eventually, I'll sift through the papers and process everything, but in the meantime, it looks terrible, and it stresses me out to see it every day. The simple act of adding new papers to that pile soon becomes a habit.

Most unwanted habits can be eliminated by simply changing our behavior. Sometimes that's easy to do, such as in the examples above, but sometimes it's harder. When we notice that we're struggling to shift an unwanted habit, it's time to stop and take a look at our mindset.

What are we afraid of? What are our beliefs about these tasks? I once worked with a client who was behind in doing her tax return. She had boxes and boxes of receipts and paperwork, but she couldn't bear the thought of going through everything. She knew it wouldn't take more than a couple of days to sort through, but she was afraid of what she'd find. And she was scared of how much tax she would owe. Eventually, we did some mindset shifts that made it easier for her to get through the stack of papers, and it was a massive relief. She owed much less than she feared, and she was able to set up more supportive habits for the following tax year.

The easiest way to release these stubborn habits is to change your beliefs. Figure out what you're currently doing that doesn't serve you, and what you'd rather have instead. Then, do the mindset work to make the changes you need to make to have a mindset full of beliefs that support you. You'll learn more about how to do that in later chapters.

## Watch your habits, for they become your character

If your habits are made up of the actions that you've taken so many times that they've become almost involuntary, then your character is made up of your unique collection of habits, among other things. The saying goes that actions speak louder than words, and this is especially true in this case. You may think that your mindset is in good shape, but if your actions prove otherwise, then you need to take a look at how your beliefs are influencing your character. I'm sure you've heard the saying: don't pay attention to what people say; pay attention to what they *do*. What do *your* habits say about *you*?

I once knew an entrepreneur who believed himself to be a charismatic and creative leader in his company, but his actions proved him to be an insufferable tyrant. Employee morale was terrible, despite his enthusiastic pep talks. He regularly and consistently micromanaged people (or bullied his managers into doing it for him), and he erupted into tantrums whenever things didn't go his way. These weren't random situations, but consistent and recurring events that eventually showed most people that this was simply the way he was—despite his belief to the contrary.

On the other end of the spectrum, I used to be painfully quiet and shy. This shyness went way back to my school years, where I dreaded being called upon by teachers to answer a question. I would go out of my way to avoid eye contact, even when I knew the answer. I just didn't want to be the center of attention. This quietness continued throughout elementary school into high school, university, and even grad school. I was good at taking tests and writing papers, but I dreaded any kind of verbal participation in class.

The more I avoided it, the worse it got. It wasn't until I joined Toastmasters in 2011—a public speaking club—that not only did I get over my fear of speaking, but I began to enjoy it. It didn't take long before I started to seek out speaking opportunities.

You may believe yourself to be a budding online entrepreneur destined for success, but if you're struggling to send out emails to your list or write a new blog post, you might want to consider what's going on. You can most definitely transform yourself into a successful online business owner, but you're probably going to have to do some work on your beliefs first.

## Watch your character, for it becomes your destiny

Destiny often refers to fate or a predetermined and unavoidable course of events. I don't believe in fate or destiny, so for our purposes, let's look at it as the power that determines a sequence of events: let's explore your "destiny" as a successful entrepreneur or business owner. Can you see how your character, which is made up of your thoughts (beliefs), words, actions, and habits, directly influences your ability to create a successful business (or not)?

When you do the mindset work to overcome the fears, blocks, and limiting beliefs that are keeping you stuck, it makes it so much easier to take action—which is what eventually gets you results in your business. At the same time that you release limiting beliefs, it's essential to reprogram your mindset with new beliefs that support you in your business vision. When your business beliefs are aligned with your business goals, action-taking is easy and effortless.

When I used to work with clients, we would dig deep to identify which beliefs were holding them back, and then we changed those beliefs, replacing them with positive, supportive beliefs. We would do work at both the subconscious and energetic levels to create profound, lasting change. At the end of each session, we would create an action plan that involved taking real-life, practical business action toward their goals. When I work with myself, I follow the same process: identify current beliefs, transform them, take action.

In changing your beliefs, you change your destiny. It's that simple.

**Take action today**

Can you think of examples of how your thoughts—perhaps in the form of mind gremlins—became spoken words that weren't very nice? And can you see how those words influenced your actions, which may have later become habits? Can you see how each of these steps may have affected your character? And finally, can you think of examples of how your words, actions, habits, and character have negatively impacted your business?

**On the podcast**

You can find the full list of podcast episodes here: www.hollyworton.com/podcast

- 306 Holly Worton ~ How To Create New Habits That Last
- 197 Holly Worton ~ Step into Your Greatness by Upgrading Your Business Beliefs
- 192 Holly Worton ~ Get the Mindset You Need to Make a Big Impact

# ABOUT THE AUTHOR

Holly Worton is a podcaster and nine times published author. Her 2019 book, *If Trees Could Talk: Life Lessons from the Wisdom of the Woods*, went straight to the top of 16 Amazon bestseller lists, and she has been featured on BBC Radio Scotland and on prime time national television in the UK – on ITV's This Morning.

She helps people get to know themselves better through connecting with Nature, so they can feel happier and more fulfilled. Holly enjoys spending time outdoors, walking long-distance trails and exploring Britain's sacred sites. She's originally from California and now lives in the Surrey Hills, but has also lived in Spain, Costa Rica, Mexico, Chile, and Argentina. Holly is a member of the Druid order OBOD.

Holly ran her first business for ten years, building it up to become a multi-million-dollar enterprise. When she went into the coaching world she was confident that she had the business and marketing skills she needed to set up a new company. And she did – but she struggled to grow her new venture quickly because she encountered fears, blocks, and limiting beliefs that she didn't even know she had.

She discovered that pushing forward and taking action just wasn't enough. She needed to transform her mindset and release her blocks, as this was the only way to take the *right* actions to move her new business forward. Thus began her journey of intense personal development through deep mindset work, which transformed her existing coaching business into a focus on helping people with their business mindset.

Eventually, she realized that she wanted to devote her time to helping people through her writing, and she let go of her mindset business to focus on her books. Now, Holly continues to write about mindset, long-distance walking, and connecting to Nature.

## Podcast

You can find her podcast on Apple Podcasts, or wherever you listen to podcasts. Links to subscribe, as well as the full list of episodes, can be found here: http://www.hollyworton.com/podcast/.

## Patreon

You can join her online community where you can receive the benefits of her done-for-you mindset work, and also get discounts on one-to-one sessions, by joining her on Patreon: https://www.patreon.com/hollyworton.

## Books

You can find her other books, including her books on nature, walking long-distance trails and business mindset, wherever you purchased this book.

## Newsletter

Finally, you can stay in touch by subscribing to her newsletter on her main website: http://www.hollyworton.com/.

amazon.com/author/hollyworton

facebook.com/HollyWortonPage

twitter.com/hollyworton

instagram.com/hollyworton

goodreads.com/HollyWorton

bookbub.com/profile/holly-worton

## ALSO BY HOLLY E. WORTON

### Business Mindset series

*Business Beliefs: Upgrade Your Mindset to Overcome Self Sabotage, Achieve Your Goals, and Transform Your Business (and Life)*

*Business Beliefs: A Companion Workbook*

*Business Blocks: Transform Your Self-Sabotaging Mind Gremlins, Awaken Your Inner Mentor, and Allow Your Business Brilliance to Shine*

*Business Blocks: A Companion Workbook*

*Business Intuition: Tools to Help You Trust Your Own Instincts, Connect with Your Inner Compass, and Easily Make the Right Decisions*

*Business Intuition: A Companion Workbook*

*Business Visibility: A Companion Workbook*

### Into the Woods Short Reads

*How to Add More Adventure to Your Life*

*How to Practice Self-Love: Actual Steps You Can Take To Love Yourself More*

*How to Practice Self Care: Even When You Think You're Too Busy*

*How to Develop Your Own Inner Compass: Learn to Trust Yourself and Easily Make the Best Decisions*

## Nature books

*If Trees Could Talk: Life Lessons from the Wisdom of the Woods*

*If Trees Could Talk: Life Lessons from the Wisdom of the Woods — A Companion Workbook*

## Walking books

*Alone on the South Downs Way: A Tale of Two Journeys from Winchester to Eastbourne*

*Walking the Downs Link: Planning Guide & Reflections on Walking from St. Martha's Hill to Shoreham-by-Sea*

*Alone on the Ridgeway: One Woman's Solo Journey from Avebury to Ivinghoe Beacon*

*Walking the Wey-South Path: Planning Guide & Reflections on Walking from Guildford to Amberley*

## A REQUEST

If you enjoyed this book, please review it online. It takes just a couple of minutes to write a quick review. It would mean the world to me! Good reviews help other readers to discover new books.

Thank you, thank you, thank you.